THE CRISIS OF UNEMPLOYMENT

Christopher Helm Vital Issues Series
Series editor: Geoffrey Alderman

Racism in Britain
Brian D. Jacobs

THE CRISIS OF UNEMPLOYMENT

ALAN GORDON

CHRISTOPHER HELM
London

© 1988 Alan Gordon
Christopher Helm (Publishers) Ltd, Imperial House,
21–25 North Street, Bromley, Kent BR1 1SD

ISBN 0-7470-1215-6 Hbk
ISBN 0-7470-1216-4 Pbk

A CIP catalogue record for this book
is available from the British Library

Typeset by Florencetype Ltd, Kewstoke, Avon
Printed and bound in Great Britain by
Billing and Sons Ltd, Worcester

CONTENTS

To Pam and Henry

List of Figures

List of Tables

'Economic policy should not be a matter of tearing up by the roots, but of slowly training a plant to grow in a different direction.'

John Maynard Keynes

'You have not been forgotten, you will not be forgotten. For that you have my word.'

Lord Young's Message to
the Unemployed

Preface

Not long after the election of Margaret Thatcher's first government in 1979, it was commented that living with Thatcherism might not be much fun, but it was certain to be an invigorating intellectual experience, especially so if you did not happen to live in the United Kingdom.

For the millions of people who have lost their jobs, as part of the Thatcher economic experiment, life has been neither fun nor a profound intellectual exercise. For them it has resulted in increasing poverty and a deterioration in physical and mental health. Of particular concern is the lot of the 1.3 million people who have been out of work for over a year. One in nine children is living in a family where the head of the household is unemployed. There is a crisis of unemployment in the UK not seen since the 1930s. The present Conservative government does not even seem interested in finding a solution. It does, after all, have much more important policy measures to pursue—privatisation of the public utilities, tinkering with education, introducing a poll tax. It is not too strong to consider these measures as an irrelevancy, given that 4 million citizens of the UK are jobless.

The stimulus to write this book came from an awareness that unemployment was becoming a forgotten policy issue in the late 1980s. A certain complacency and resignation was setting in. Month after month and year after year unemployment at 3 million or thereabouts was meriting less and less attention and concern. In spite of the numbers involved and the deprivation experienced by those out of work, those with jobs and often experiencing rising living standards did not seem to care. The Thatcherite outlook of individualism, self-help and the 'bootstrap and bicycle' mentality has become fairly pervasive. The 87 per cent of us in work need continually reminding that the jobless are still there, with motivations, hopes, fears, spouses, children and debts.

This book aims to provide a lively, well-informed and easily understandable explanation of the problem of unemployment, its causes and possible remedies. The book is aimed at the intelligent layperson, interested in what is without doubt the most serious problem facing the UK in the 1980s and 1990s. And it does have to be faced up to. No specialist knowledge or education is required to understand this book, although it does not make happy or cheerful bedside reading.

Acknowledgements

I am grateful to those who helped me in the most formative stages of my learning curve: Alan Maynard, Mike Cooper, Roy Parker, Gareth Williams and Richard Pearson. I am still learning. None of them read this book in advance of publication, and it is at least possible they will now deny ever having known me!

Thank you to those who encouraged me to finish this book in time to avoid being castigated by Richard Wigmore at Christopher Helm. Special thanks to my wife Pam, who has been supportive and enthusiastic throughout. The island of Corsica provided a brief respite in the summer of 1987, allowing me time to collect my thoughts before embarking on the final bout of writing, refreshed and keen.

Special thanks is due to Jan Cadge who, once again, provided efficient and uncomplaining secretarial support throughout.

The book, however, is my own.

Alan Gordon
Royal Holloway and Bedford New College
University of London

1. Introduction: Crisis? What Crisis?

In August 1987 the official figure for adult unemployment had been falling for no less than fourteen consecutive months. Up to 40,000 people a month were leaving the dole queues. Although the official unemployment count for August still stood as high as 2.9 million, this was over 400,000 fewer than the peak level of unemployment in the United Kingdom in the 1980s.

Surely, then, this is sufficient reason for thinking that the crisis of unemployment has now abated, that the turning-point has been reached and passed, and that at long last we have returned to the path of fuller employment. Have the Thatcherites been correct all along, then, in their view of the causes of our high unemployment, and similarly correct in some, if not all, of the remedies pursued? Are we now seeing the benefits to unemployment of a greater flexibility in the labour market, an erosion of the power of trade unions, tax-cuts and public-spending constraint, action on welfare benefits, and an expansion of special schemes for the unemployed? After all, there are more people in jobs; we have witnessed a large increase in self-employment; and there is the success of government training and retraining measures. All the informed talk, at least up until the time of the Stock Exchange crash in October 1987, was of high economic growth and a consumer boom. The good times have returned, or at least are returning to United Kingdom plc.

Or are they? Is unemployment still the most serious and economic problem facing the country? Is the scale of human waste and misery still of crisis proportions? It is, and for many, many reasons.

The figure of 2.9 million unemployed is unrealistically low. In 1987 there were over 700,000 unemployed people on government special schemes or holding their 'jobs' with the assistance of job subsidies. This help is temporary. A sharp expansion in special employment measures in 1986 and 1987 has had the effect of massaging the government unemployment figures substantially downwards. For example, 65,000 more young people were on the Youth Training Scheme (YTS) in 1987 than in the summer of 1986. In addition, since 1979 there have been no less than nineteen changes made to the way the unemployed are officially counted each month. If we still defined the unemployed in the way that the government did in 1979 (when 'only' 1.3 million people were out of work) this would add over 500,000 more people to the dole queue. So, even when adult unemployment has been falling for over a year, the real level of unemployment is still over 4 million people. The scale of the problem remains immense, something recognised in every public-opinion poll, which show unemployment as the most severe economic problem confronting the nation.

But perhaps the lot of the unemployed will be getting better and better in the late 1980s and in the 1990s? The haul-back may have been excruciatingly slow, and severely painful for those bearing the brunt of it, but now that economic policies are starting to work (the argument runs), are the most recent trends not a source of optimism for the future? They are not. Groups as diverse as the International Monetary Fund, the Confederation of British Industry and the Organisation for Economic Co-operation and Development all expect the fall in British unemployment to cease in 1988. Indeed, a further increase is on the cards. And this was before the stock exchange crashes around the world in October 1987 started off another round of forecasts of recession and rising unemployment in 1988 and beyond, caused by the deflationary effects of the crash. Longer-term forecasts of the labour market show a continued loss of jobs in manufacturing, only partly compensated for by increases in service jobs. Without a shift in policy there is little hope of the official unemployment count deviating much from present levels. And it may go higher still. The UK then, is stuck on a plateau of a real level of unemployment at the 4-million mark, with little prospect of a substantial cut in the jobless in the foreseeable future. On the basis of existing policies, the crisis of unemployment will remain into the mid-1990s. And the years 1986 and 1987 were the good times. In comparison with the experiences of the deep world recession of the early 1980s to October 1987, economic growth is high, inflation is low, international trade is buoyant, world commodity prices are relatively low, and sterling is stable. But unemployment remains sticky at 4 million. With the onset of a further trough in the economic cycle we may look back fondly to the days when registered unemployment was just 13 per cent!

This is a far cry from the years when the maintenance of full employment was the single most important objective of government. For most of the period since 1945 unemployment was substantially below 5 per cent, reaching a low of just over 1 per cent in the mid-1950s. In the 1960s and 1970s unemployment did tend to rise, but it was a slow process. The consensus and commitment was to keep as near to full employment as could be attained, regardless of the colours of the political party in power. Historically, full employment can be considered as an unemployment rate of 3 per cent or less. For 1987 and 1988 this would produce an unemployment count of some 800,000 unemployed people (see Chapter 2). The election of the first Thatcher government in 1979 represented a fundamental, stepwise shift in economic policy-making on a number of fronts, the most important of which has been the total abandonment of any kind of commitment to full employment.

The main priority of the Thatcher government was to squeeze domestically produced inflation out of the system. If this caused high unemployment, so be it. The fact that such deflationary policies began to be applied at the same time as world recessionary pressures were leading to higher unemployment and lower inflation anyway, just made matters worse still. The economic policies that in the previous thirty-five years had been used to counter recession were discarded. In their stead, we initially imported a brand of monetarism from across the Atlantic, based on nineteenth-century theories of how money moves in the economy. The government chose to try and free-up markets, including the labour market, and adopted a supply-sider interpretation of the causes of unemployment. The acceptance of these causes, such as low labour quality, high wages, overly generous benefits, penalising rates of income tax and an oversized public sector, inevitably led to the adoption of policies aimed at counteracting these malfunctions and distortions in the market place. Unemployment then trebled from its 1979 level of 1.3 million.

There remains a continuing debate among economists and policy-makers about the causes of the UK's high unemployment. In this country, unemployment rose more quickly and to higher levels earlier and then stuck, in comparison with most other developed countries. This experience has to be explained. Blaming the welfare-benefits system, the trade unions and the world recession is just not good enough (see Chapter 3). Indeed, if this analysis of causes were correct, then after the enthusiastic pursuit of policies specifically designed to remove these impediments for eight full years, we really should have been reaping the benefits of this before 1987 in the form of substantially lower unemployment. The policies cannot work, because the analysis of just what has caused the present crisis of unemployment is fundamentally flawed. Seventy per cent of the increase in unemployment in the UK has been caused by a lack of demand in the economy. To counteract the malaise of unemployment requires expansionary policies at home, targeted on those groups feeling the effects of unemployment most severely, and those most at risk of losing their jobs.

We can identify just who are the unemployed and those most likely to lose their jobs. The duration of unemployment is clearly a problem: while every month hundreds of thousands of people find jobs, hundreds of thousands also lose theirs. There is a daily, weekly, and monthly flow off and on the unemployment register. Particularly disadvantaged are the official stock of 1.3 million people who have been unemployed for over a year. One in five of the unemployed has been out of work for three years or longer (Chapter 4). The government special employment and training measures are puny in comparison with the scale of the problem. Where you live and what you do for a living has become increasingly important in the 1980s. Job losses have been concentrated in the regions furthest from the south-east. In 1987 unemployment is now below 4 per cent in many towns in the south-east. Indeed, the levels of unemployment in some parts of the south, when at their worst, have been lower than those experienced by parts of the north, Scotland, Wales and Northern Ireland during the boom years. It remains at 20 per cent and over elsewhere. The variations in unemployment can be generalised into a North–South divide, but a closer scrutiny of local employment opportunities and unemployment rates is more rewarding in assessing differences across the country—the gap is widening and on present policies will widen still further in the 1990s.

The local and regional differences partly reflect the reliance of different areas on particular types of employment. Especially severe has been the loss of jobs in manufacturing, construction and the primary industries (e.g. coal); and these losses will continue. It was only in the autumn of 1987 that manufacturing output reached the levels obtained in 1979, but with nearly 2 million fewer employees. Those in semi-skilled and unskilled jobs are nearly five times more likely to experience unemployment than those doing professional work.

First targets for an employment regeneration programme then, have to include the long-term unemployed, those out of work in high-unemployment areas, those with few or no skills, and those formerly relying on non-service-sector employers for work. There are, of course, overlaps. With the focus of attention for unemployment alleviation on these groups, the high unemployment and social and economic deprivations of the inner cities will inevitably be included. High unemployment among the ethnic minorities will also be a target for ameliorative measures in this way. Youth unemployment is a problem for all ethnic groups, but black teenagers experience an unemployment rate close to 40 per cent. This has to change.

Because the experience of unemployment is not evenly distributed among the population, the 'corrosive effects' of unemployment remain an unknown quantity for many, too. The evidence now is overwhelming—extended periods of unemployment lead to poverty and a sharp deterioration in physical and mental health (Chapter 5). Proposals on further benefit reforms emanating from the Conservative Party in late 1987 would lead to even more people being sucked into poverty, more quickly and to greater depths. Yet all the policy changes on benefits since 1979 have been to this effect already: cuts in benefits and further restrictions on the eligibility of claimants. The evidence of the impact of unemployment on physical and mental health comes from a variety of sources, and all point in the same direction. Loss of a job is debilitating in its effects; it can be devastating, even fatal. Attempted suicide is more common, and the risk of death from 'natural causes' including heart disease increases. Any caring society would recognise the profound risk to the health of its citizens presented by unemployment, and would instigate an emergency back-to-work programme. At present the government, and many of the 87 per cent of us in work, are both ignorant of and ignore their plight.

The severe problems of the unemployed are not peculiar to those out of work in the UK. Other countries too have had to face up to unprecedentedly high unemployment in the 1980s. In Germany, for those eligible for unemployment benefits, material deprivation is somewhat less of a problem. In the USA federal and state programmes do assist the unemployed with training and employment creation. The UK government has been carefully scrutinising US 'workfare' policies with a view to their widespread introduction this side of the Atlantic. (Workfare is where the unemployed, and other groups, are engaging in community work of some kind to 'earn' their benefits.) Australia, over the past decade, has used a wide variety of special measures to assist their own unemployed, including public-sector job creation, special training programmes and job subsidies. Maybe there are some lessons for the UK in the way other countries have responded to high unemployment in the 1980s. The USA has experienced the most dramatic fall in the numbers unemployed and increase in the number of new jobs created. In 1987 unemployment in the USA fell to below 6 per cent, and over 9 million new jobs have been created. Was this achieved by the earnest pursuit of the policies adopted in the UK? Of course not. In spite of protestations to the contrary, the US success in job creation and cutting unemployment has been achieved through increasing government spending and cutting taxes, thus stimulating the US economy to produce jobs. It has been estimated that up to 50 per cent of the increase in US unemployment in the early 1980s was caused by a deficiency in demand in the economy. The adoption of reflationary policies in 1987 dramatically reversed the trend.

The criticism of the US way is that the scale of its imbalance between spending and revenue (the budget deficit) has been entirely imprudent. A gap of $200 billion was clearly unsustainable. We all discovered this in October 1987 with the so-called 'Black Monday' on stock exchanges around the world. The US trade deficit did not help either.

Other industrialised countries have attempted to alleviate unemployment with a range of special measures, often aimed at particularly disadvantaged groups such as young unemployed people, or in the case of Australia, the Aboriginal population. Certainly, in the UK, special employment and training measures have grown in scope and scale enormously in the 1980s (Chapter 7). The two largest are the Youth Training Scheme (YTS), for 16- and 17-year-olds, and the Community Programme, which is mainly work-creation for the long-term unemployed. There are also job subsidies for 18- to 20-year-olds and the long-term unemployed. Over 700,000 people are now assisted by special measures in one way or another. As noted above, they are also removed from the official unemployment count. A relative newcomer to the armoury of special initiatives is the Job Training Scheme, aiming eventually to train 250,000 people a year. Participants receive just their normal unemployment or supplementary benefit while on this scheme (they may also be eligible for assistance with travel expenses), but no additional training allowance is paid. The Job Training Scheme is the closest the UK has come yet to workfare, although near-compulsion to take part in one special scheme or another following a 'Restart' interview, with the threat of a loss of benefit if the offer is declined, makes the 'workfare' description of the country's special measures more accurate than ever before. The government's intention is to make the YTS compulsory in 1988 for those not in a job and not staying on in education. 'No YTS no money' will be the order of the day from 1988. The *Action for Jobs* booklet lists 26 different schemes.

These schemes offer temporary relief for some; but they are essentially palliatives, acting on symptoms rather than on the main causes of high unemployment. Special measures of different kinds, particularly when targeted at those groups of people most adversely affected by unemployment clearly have some role to play in the fight back against the crisis of unemployment. Improved and forward-looking training and retraining is necessary for some groups to regain their rightful and active place in the labour force. Employers may need some special incentives to recruit the long-term unemployed in preference to job-changers. But the careful targeting of such measures is necessary. More important is the whole thrust of government economic policy. The Conservative government's view of the economy as a ruler rather than an elastic band is simplistic and naïve. Their approach to the role of the state in job creation, as in other things such as education and health care, is ideologically based and has little to do with economics. A job in the public services can be 'bought' by government for little more in the way of net cost than maintaining somebody on the dole.

The 1980s have seen a range of alternative policies on unemployment put forward by economists, policy-makers and the political parties (Chapter 8). Some have been fairly conventional in approach, arguing for expansionist job-creation measures funded through government borrowing and (sometimes) increased taxation. These have a contribution to make. Other ideas are rather novel. But certainly, in attempting to relieve the misery of the unemployed no policy initiative with any likelihood of success should remain ignored. Unemployment remains the single most severe social and economic problem facing the UK. On existing policies the figure of 4 million unemployed will remain with us well into the 1990s. There *is* an alternative that will get the country back to work. Unemployment *can* be dramatically cut to 1 million. This is close to the full employment objectives proposed by Keynes and Beveridge in the 1940s. And it *is* attainable.

In 1978, before the election of the first Thatcher government, Bacon and Eltis, two economists concerned about the size of the public sector in the UK, wrote:

> there would be the certainty of disaster if a Conservative pro-market sector government came to power and just sat back, balanced the budget, and let unemployment mount, waiting for the market to solve its problems.

A decade on we have that disaster: it is the crisis of unemployment.

2. Good Times and Bad Times

In January 1933 there were 2,979,400 people unemployed in the United Kingdom. Until the 1980s this was the highest-ever total of jobless.

If one takes into account the children and wives of the unemployed (83 per cent of the unemployed in the early 1930s were men) then it is estimated that there must have been 'well over 5 million people dependent on niggardly weekly payments of a few shillings each per head' (Michael Young). At one time or another in the 1930s, over one-half of the nation's workers were involuntarily jobless. It was the experience of mass unemployment in the 1930s that led to the development and execution of a set of policies in the 1940s and afterwards, that would try to ensure that high unemployment would never again occur in the UK. Economists and politicians of all persuasions were convinced of the need to adopt policies that would get the country back to work and, once there, maintain full employment. Full employment was to be the single most important economic and social objective—until, that is, the election of the Thatcher Conservative government in 1979, which had other priorities.

The two leading figures in the 1930s and 1940s who put firmly into place the full-employment objective for the United Kingdom were William Beveridge and John Maynard Keynes. Beveridge's *Full Employment in a Free Society*, Keynes's *General Theory* and related articles and, most importantly, the 1944 White Paper on Employment Policy and associated legislation, provided the mechanism and set the tenor for employment policy for the following thirty years.

As far as Beveridge and Keynes were concerned, full employment meant having not more than 3 per cent of the labour force unemployed at any time. The reason why full employment was not (and could not be) considered to be zero per cent unemployment is because of the existence of frictional unemployment (see also Chapter 3). Beveridge and Keynes recognised that because of people changing jobs and because of the process of job search for new entrants to the labour market, unemployment could not be zero per cent. In addition, structural changes are continually taking place in the economy, with the decline and demise of old industries and the development and growth of new ones, and with old skills becoming redundant and new skills having to be learnt by displaced workers. For these reasons, in the main, it was considered extremely difficult, if not impossible, for any government with any set of economic and social policies, to reduce unemployment below 3 per cent.

Historically, then, full employment was considered to be about 3 per cent of the labour force unemployed at any time. In the 1940s this would represent some 500,000 people out of work. With the rather larger labour force of the 1980s (over 27 million) 3 per cent unemployment in 1987 would be an unemployment count of 800,000.

Beveridge went well beyond just stating that unemployment should not increase beyond 3 per cent. His fully employed society was one where those who did lose their jobs, or who were looking for work for the first time (for example, school leavers) should be able to find new jobs at fair wages 'without delay'. Beveridge considered two months or so to be an appropriate maximum time to be without a job. In addition, the stated policy objective was that ideally there should always be more job vacancies than there were unemployed people looking for jobs. These job vacancies should also be geographically distributed in such a way that the unemployed could take them up. They should have skill needs and pay levels that match the requirements of the unemployed. These objectives, that were to be strived for, were a far cry from present experiences. There is currently a dramatic mismatch between the types of job vacancies available and the skills of the unemployed over and above the vast numerical mismatch between vacancies and unemployment numbers. The regional problem further compounds the difficulty.

What Beveridge and Keynes provided, following the experiences of the depression years of the 1930s, was a set of policy objectives that should be vigorously pursued to ensure that there could be no return to mass unemployment. They also gave us the economic and social policies that would deliver on these objectives. But perhaps the greatest achievement was the development of a consensus, among economists and politicians alike, that the foremost objective of government was to manage the economy in a way that would ensure full employment.

In the 1950s and up until the mid-1960s unemployment was even lower than Keynes and Beveridge considered possible. During this period unemployment averaged under 2 per cent. Although rising slowly, unemployment was kept below 4 per cent in the later 1960s, reaching 4 per cent in the early 1970s. In 1971 there were 751,000 unemployed people claiming benefit, but by 1976 this figure had risen to 1.3 million, or over 6 per cent of the labour force (employed and unemployed). Unemployment stood at 1.3 million at the time of the election of the Conservative government in 1979. Registered unemployment reached 3 million three years later and by mid-1986 stood at 3.3 million. There have now been 19 changes since 1979 to the way that the unemployed are counted, which makes tracking precisely what has been happening in the 1980s somewhat problematic. The number of changes is to increase to 21. Fortunately, an organisation called the Unemployment Unit have set themselves the task, along with many other things, of putting the unemployment figures in 1987 and 1988 on a footing comparable with earlier years. This is discussed in more detail below.

So, even according to the government's own figures, an additional 2 million people were added to the dole queue between 1979 and 1986. The real figure is much higher. The causes of this increase are subject to some dispute (see Chapter 3) but we do have to distinguish between some of the longer-term causes that led to an increase in the unemployment rate from under 2 per cent in the 1950s to 5 to 6 per cent in the late 1970s, and the causes of the sharp increase experienced since 1979.

For the longer term, factors such as productivity and competitiveness, investment (private and public), outmoded working practices, perhaps complacency, poor management and de-industrialisation may all have contributed. The increase in unemployment that occurred between 1974 and 1976 was caused in large part by the first oil-price increase and the ensuing world recession. But remember, unemployment only increased to 1.3 million during this period. The second oil-price increase was associated with (and is blamed by some for) the sharp rise in unemployment between 1980 and 1982. The UK was, of course, a major oil producer in its own right by this time. And by the late 1980s we also have some experience of lower oil prices once again.

The year 1979 saw a stepwise change in the objectives of government. Until this time, however unsuccessfully for some periods, governments from 1945 to 1979 had as an ideal the pursuit of high-employment and low-unemployment policies. The consensus forged by Beveridge and Keynes in the early 1940s had held, and even if there was an inability to deliver full employment, there is no doubting that as an objective it stood totem-like before every Prime Minister and Secretary of State for Employment. The election of the first Thatcher government in 1979 took a hatchet to this totem. There is no longer any commitment to high employment, let alone full employment.

The adoption of a supposedly less interventionist stance in the economy (although it can be argued that the Conservative government is as strongly interventionist as its predecessors, but in a different way with different priorities), together with its acceptance that it is the poor workings of an inflexible labour market that give rise to high unemployment, have led to a downgrading of the importance of unemployment as an economic and social problem to be tackled. In particular, inflation was seen as a greater evil than unemployment, and if the deflationary policies singlemindedly pursued to cure inflation actually led to hundreds of thousands losing their jobs, so be it. In addition, the acceptance of monetarism as an economic philosophy meant that a government would try to control only what it thought it could control. So, it would try to control the amount of money in the economy, it would be strongly interventionist on interest rates, and it would attempt to influence the value of sterling. The government, it was believed, could not affect the level of economic activity in the country in any sustainable way: it could not provide jobs for the unemployed. As the 1985 White Paper baldly states: 'Government cannot do what the nation will not. It cannot on its own create jobs'.

Since 1979 we have witnessed the total abandonment of full-employment objectives. Government attempts to reduce inflation in the UK have been totally responsible for adding over 1.5 million people to the dole queues. There have merely been attempts to bring the labour market closer to the classical economists' dream of a perfect market. No attempts are made to manipulate taxation, public spending, exchange rates and regulations, credit and interest rates in order to put the country back to work. For the 1980s full employment is regarded as an unattainable state. There is more than a suspicion that for the government it would be an undesirable state as well. The new reality of high unemployment has not prevented there being a whole succession of changes to the way the unemployed are counted.

THE REAL LEVEL OF UNEMPLOYMENT

In September 1986 the 'official' unemployment count was given as 3,332,897, an unemployment rate of 13.5 per cent of the labour

Figure 2.1: Unemployment rate in the UK, 1971–87. Unemployed claimants as a percentage of the working population

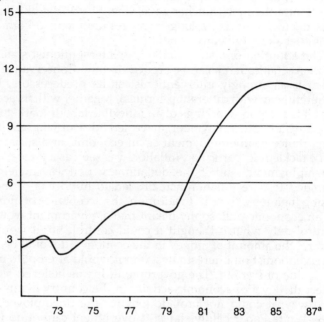

Note: a. Average of first six months, 1987.

Sources: *Social Trends*, 17; *Employment Gazette.*

force. If we still calculated unemployment in the way acceptable in 1980, the figure would have been 3,858,500, or 15.6 per cent. A new change during 1986 was that instead of the registered-claimant unemployed being expressed as a percentage of employees in employment and the unemployed being added together, now the unemployed are given as a proportion of the rather larger working population. The difference is that this working population includes an estimate for the self-employed and armed forces personnel as well as counting employees and the unemployed. This may seem like rather bothersome semantics—but the effect of using a larger denominator in this way is to shave between 1 per cent and 1.5 per cent off the published unemployment rate. So, in September 1986 the unemployed would have represented 12.1 per cent of the working population, rather less mountainous than 13.5

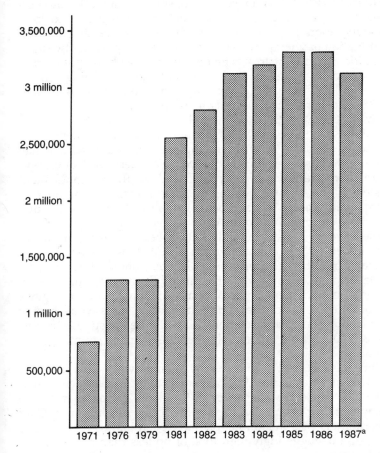

Figure 2.2: Unemployed claimants 1971–87, UK

NOTE: a. Average of first six months, 1987. The chart gives the official unemployment count. Since 1979 about half a million unemployed people have been excluded from the official figures because of the 19 changes made to the way the unemployed are counted.

Sources: *Social Trends, 17; Employment Gazette.*

per cent or 15.6 per cent! Figure 2.1 shows the unemployment rate calculated on this new basis from 1971 to 1986. Figure 2.2 shows total claimant-unemployment in each year from 1979.

At present this relatively recent method of calculating the unemployment rate is published alongside the rate calculated on the old basis. It is likely to be only a matter of time before the 'old' rate publication is abandoned, if the experience of statistical manipulation of unemployment figures over the past eight years is any guide. Already history is being rewritten with the publication of a seasonally adjusted unemployment rate (excluding school-leavers) on the new basis of working population stretching back to 1971 (Figure 2.1; see *Social Trends*, 1987 edition).

It is misleading to think of unemployment as being an immobile pool of those looking for work. The monthly unemployment count represents the stock of those unemployed on one particular day each month. However, during the course of every week and every month there are flows of people on and off the unemployment register. If the number joining is greater than the number of unemployed ceasing to claim benefit (they will not all be starting jobs) then the monthly count will increase. And if, say, 500,000 people leave the register but only 400,000 become unemployed and claim benefit, then unemployment will fall by 100,000 in that particular month. The *Employment Gazette*, published monthly by the Department of Employment, contains a good range of information on unemployment (internationally, nationally and by regions and localities), on vacancies, on redundancies and a whole host of other labour-market information. It should be consulted. In June 1987 315,000 people entered the benefit-claimant count; 403,000 left it.

While it is incorrect to consider the unemployed as this stagnant, and what at times in the 1980s appeared to be an ever deepening, pool, it is the case that over 1.3 million people have been unemployed for over a year, according to the official count. Over three-quarters of a million people have been jobless for over two years, and a staggeringly high total of no less than half a million people have been out of work for over three years. For some unemployed people to think of themselves just as a stagnant pool rather than a flow, is not so mistaken.

One or two alterations to the way the unemployed are counted over the 1980s, if it were to improve statistical accuracy, would be perfectly acceptable. Five or six changes might cause an eyebrow or two to be raised, but might be justified. But *nineteen* changes, or what the Unemployment Unit calls 'statistical sleights' can only be interpreted as deliberate fraud. Not all of the alterations are of similar effect, but only one had the effect of increasing the monthly count. This was the 1979 change to fortnightly payment of unemployment benefits, which increased the count by some 20,000 each month. The statistics were immediately compensated downwards by 20,000 to take account of this. No other correction has been made in the interests of fine-tuning the statistics to deal with all the myriad changes that have taken people off of the unemployment register.

The most important change in the way the unemployed are counted took place in 1982. This was a move from a manual count of all unemployed people to a computerised record based on benefit claimants only. This change on its own took almost 200,000 people out of unemployment, many of whom were women ineligible to claim benefit because of insufficient or low level of national insurance contributions. Men aged 60 and over were given the incentive of receiving a higher rate of benefit together with national insurance credits in return for not signing on at benefit offices (two changes), and over 160,000 older men were affected by this. The 1986 change that introduced a two-week delay in publication of the monthly unemployment count took an estimated 50,000 a month off the total. This alteration was put into effect 'to improve accuracy', of course. The other changes have each taken between 5,000 and 30,000 out of the unemployment count. Altogether over 500,000 people have been excluded from being counted as unemployed since 1979 as a result of these changes.

However, the biggest single way in which the monthly published total of unemployment is a gross underestimate of the real position is the way all those unemployed people on government special schemes for the unemployed are excluded. The numbers involved have more than doubled since 1979 and now stand at well over 700,000. Great efforts have been made in 1987, in particular, to shift people out of the unemployment count and into special employment and training measures, whether it be the YTS or the Community Programme. The compulsory attendance by the unemployed at 'Restart' interviews explicitly aims to get unemployed people onto a scheme, into self-employment or (for a tiny minority) into a job. The important thing is to get them off the unemployment register.

In the UK being out of work and looking for a job is not sufficient to be counted as unemployed. You have to be eligible for benefit and claiming it as well. But even if we take the official unemployment total as our starting point, and add to this those who have been taken out since 1979 by hook or by crook by the definitional changes that have occurred since 1979 (usually by crook), we are getting to over 3.5 million unemployed. If we then add in all of those unemployed people on special schemes, where you actually have to be unemployed to be eligible, then a conservative estimate of the real level of unemployment is over 4 million people.

Corroborating evidence for a figure of unemployment at about this level comes from the annual *Labour Force Survey* and other research. The 1984 *Survey* found 870,000 people looking for jobs who were ineligible to claim benefit, and this group clearly should be added to the official count. On the other side of the coin, there are a group of benefit claimants who do have paid work. At *most* this group numbers 200,000 and should be deducted from the official total. And we still have to add in those on special schemes. So a figure of 4 million unemployed does not appear to be an unrealistic one: if anything it errs rather on the side of an undercount. Nigel Lawson, currently Chancellor of the Exchequer, does not agree. He told the Conservative Party in conference at Blackpool in 1985 that, 'The official figures almost certainly exaggerate the true picture'.

This is arrant nonsense. But since when was a Chancellor supposed to be good at arithmetic? However, if we do accept 4 million as a reasonably accurate estimate then it makes the task of returning to high levels of employment so much more difficult. Reducing unemployment from 3 million to 1 million may appear difficult enough, but what has to be grasped is that in practice an even more heroic effort has to be made, since unemployment needs to be cut from an existing 4 million plus.

This is where the opposition parties in the United Kingdom can be accused of being rather disingenuous. While they correctly point an accusing finger at the blatant massaging of the unemployment statistics in the 1980s, in their own programmes for job-creation they are then quite happy to take the government's underestimate of the crisis of unemployment as their starting point for getting the country back to work. Personally, I cannot foresee any alternative non-Conservative government in the 1990s turning the clock back and re-imposing the old methods of calculating the unemployment total. What new Secretary of State for Employment, on assuming office in 1991 or 1992 is likely to admit that unemployment is actually over 4 million? And even if 1 million jobs were created, and even if they were all taken up by some of the 4 million, unemployment would still be at the 3-million mark. The political reality is that it just would not happen. It has to be left to those working outside the political-party machines to emphasise the scale of unemployment at every opportunity, and to set out a coherent programme to reduce unemployment from over 4 million to 1 million. Regardless of the political party in government it serves no purpose to underestimate the unemployment total. As individuals and families the unemployed will still exist, whether or not they are included in any particular, narrow, official definition. And they want jobs. For over four-fifths of the labour force, of course, this is not such a problem: they have jobs already. But those with jobs are not evenly distributed around the country.

THE NORTH–SOUTH DIVIDE

One of the major, and most serious, omissions from the 1985 government White Paper on employment policy, '*Employment: The*

Challenge of the Nation' is that it almost completely ignores regional inequalities in employment, unemployment and job loss. Increasingly, the most severe economic and social problem facing the country is not just unemployment *itself*, but rather the local and regional differences in unemployment and re-employment opportunities, and the ever widening gap between some localities and others. It is all too easy to forget that even in the depths of the early 1980s recession, some parts of the country (mainly in the south) were experiencing unemployment rates that would have been the envy of some northern, Welsh and Scottish towns and cities at the height of the boom times. At the local level now, in 1987, the official unemployment rate ranges from under 4 per cent of the labour force to over 30 per cent. Unemployment in Merseyside is fives times as high as unemployment in Crawley. Unemployment in Strabane is more than six times higher than in Guildford. Table 2.1 gives details of unemployment in some selected parts of the country.

Table 2.1: Examples of unemployment rates[a] in different parts of the country in June 1987

Winners		Losers	
Crawley	3.7	Strabane	33.9
Winchester	4.0	Cookstown	30.9
Guildford	4.6	Newry	30.2
Tunbridge Wells	4.6	South Tyneside	23.7
Cambridge	4.8	Fishguard	22.9
Newbury	4.8	Irvine	22.6
Oxford	5.0	Arbroath	21.6
Devizes	5.7	Dumbarton	20.7
Hertford	5.9	Rotherham	20.3
Hitchin	6.5	Aberdare	20.1
Harrogate	6.7	Middlesborough	20.0
Cheltenham	6.7	Liverpool	19.9
Bedford	6.9	South Pembroke	19.9
Ipswich	7.0	Sunderland	19.5
Chippenham	7.1	Redruth	19.2
Trowbridge	7.3	Penzance	16.9
Northampton	7.5	Newquay	16.8
Worcester	8.7	Hull	14.7
Bristol	9.1	Mansfield	14.7
Brighton	9.4	Birmingham	13.9

Note: a. Unemployed as percentage of civilian labour force.

Certainly, there are parts of the south and east that have unemployment rates comparable to the high unemployment of other regions. It is too simplistic to consider the country split up into the low-*unemployment* south and the low-*employment* north. However, those areas with the lowest unemployment of all are the exclusive preserve of south-east England. So, it is not only the total of unemployment that has to be rectified, attempts must also be made to affect the distribution of employment. This is no easy task.

Figures show that in the north of Britain alone more than 1 million jobs were lost in the seven years from 1979. In the south over the same period there was a 350,000 net increase in the number of jobs. One-third of manufacturing jobs in Wales and the north of England were lost during this time. Manufacturing industry suffered the most intensely as a result of government monetarist anti-inflationary policies in the early 1980s. As a result it was those regions and localities that were (and in many cases still are) dependent on manufacturing industry for employment that have suffered the highest levels of redundancy and unemployment.

Those parts of the country relying more on the services for jobs (such as the south-east and East Anglia) have been more successful in the 1980s. As the Charter for Jobs's own analysis has shown,

> Government economic policy must take its share of the blame both for the total decline in employment and for the increase in regional disparities. By placing most of the burden of economic adjustment on manufacturing industry it was inevitable that the North would suffer more than the South.

This issue of regional differences and divisions received a great deal of attention early in 1987, following the rather tardy publication of the 1984 *Census of Employment*. The Census revealed that 94 per cent of the jobs lost in Britain since the June 1979 election were north of a line drawn between the Bristol Channel in the south-west and The Wash in the east. Just 6 per cent of the job losses occurred in southern England. The contrast becomes even sharper once the self-employed are excluded. The Census figures actually showed that regional differences in the official unemployment count actually understate the increasing gap between the south-east and the rest of the country. Table 2.2 shows how the civilian employed labour force (employees in employment and self-employment) changed for each of Great Britain's regions between 1979 and 1986, and within this from 1983 to 1986. More than anything else this table shows the stark differences between regions in the Thatcher years. While the figures for 1983 to 1986 in Table 2.2 do show all but one region exhibiting plus (+) signs in the size of the labour force, this was of course from an incredibly low

Table 2.2: Changes in the civilian employed labour force[a], Great Britain

Region	Change[b] 1979–86		Change[b] 1983–6	
	Number	%	Number	%
South-east	+172,000	+2	+48,400	+6
East Anglia	+101,000	+13	+100,000	+13
South-west	+83,000	+5	+99,000	+6
West Midlands	−173,000	−7	+90,000	+4
East Midlands	+6,000	(−)	+94,000	+6
Yorkshire and Humberside	−130,000	−6	+74,000	+4
North-west	−349,000	−12	+15,000	+1
North	−138,000	−10	+39,000	+3
Wales	−145,000	−13	−2,000	(−)
Scotland	−172,000	−8	+12,000	+1

Notes: a. The civilian employed labour force adds together employees in employment *and* the self-employed.
b. June to June.

base in 1983. Rather more significant are the changes spanning the whole 1979 to 1986 period. The total figures for job losses in Table 2.2 look much better because of the inclusion of the self-employed in the civilian labour force: job losses of 745,000 since 1979 look relatively small in comparison with the employees-only figures given in Table 2.3. Between June 1979 and June 1986 there was a net decline of 1.57 million jobs. An increase of 861,000 service jobs (many part-time) went some small way towards making good the 28 per cent tumble in manufacturing jobs—a fall of a staggering 1,968,000. If one excludes the self-employed, then the north-west had a loss of 16 per cent of its jobs (415,000) and Wales lost 17 per cent of its own (175,000). Wales and the north-west lost service-industry jobs as well as manufacturing ones. And the north-west, Wales and Yorkshire and Humberside lost 35 per cent of their manufacturing jobs under the Thatcher government.

Given such massive disparities in job losses, prevailing unemployment rates and in vacancies, it makes no sense to pretend that two nations are really one. It may be the case that the country cannot be conveniently divided into a rich south and a poor north: after all, unemployment in some London boroughs and in other towns, cities and rural areas in the south exceeds 20 per cent. 'But for the average person in the North, the undeniable fact is that the chances of becoming unemployed over the last seven years have been significantly higher than for the average person in the South' (Charter for Jobs).

Table 2.3: Job losses in regions, 1979–83 and 1983–6 (employees)

Region	Changes 1979–83	Changes 1983–6
South-east	−391,000	+269,000
East Anglia	−15,000	+74,000
South-west	−84,000	+54,000
West Midlands	−298,000	+78,000
East Midlands	−132,000	+91,000
Yorks and Humber	−240,000	+5,000
North-west	−374,000	−41,000
North	−191,000	+20,000
Wales	−145,000	−30,000
Scotland	−204,000	−12,000
Great Britain	−2,074,000	+508,000

If the conclusion of a 1987 discussion paper from Cambridge University's Department of Land Economy materialises, then the period to 1995 will be marked by a reinforcement of existing marked regional inequalities. Tyler and Rhodes found that a forecast increase nationally in employment of 900,000 jobs 1985–95, almost half will be in the south-east. All national employment growth is expected to be in the private-services sector, while public-service and manufacturing employment are expected to continue their decline. The Cambridge economists urge that regional policy measures be adopted that divert some of the new jobs growth to the north, 'giving the North of this increasingly divided country a job boost which it surely deserves'. A joint report from Cambridge Econometrics and the Northern Ireland Research Centre in October 1987 forecast that the north, north-west and Northern Ireland will continue to lose jobs and population right through to the end of the century.

PEOPLE IN WORK

The total labour force or 'working population' in Great Britain numbers 27 million people. This includes employees in employment, the self-employed, those in the armed forces and the unemployed. Sixteen million men and 11 million women are in the labour force. Since 1971 the labour force has grown by 1.7 million, mainly attributable to an increased number of women working or seeking jobs. Of the 24 million in employment, 14 million are men and 10 million are women. Nearly three-quarters of those with work are in the private sector of the economy. Indeed, the number of employees in the public sector, such as the health service, central and local government and so on, has fallen from 7.3 million in 1976 to 6.6 million in 1985.

There are some quirky reasons that account for part of this fall, however, including the privatisation of some public-sector corporations. For example, the move of British Telecom from the public to private sector in November 1984 added 3 per cent to private-sector employment, and reduced public-sector employment equivalently. Public-sector employment peaked, in fact, in 1979.

The total number of *employees* in employment rose by over 1 million in the 1970s, then fell to 1983. The total number of employees now stands at 21.5 million (see Table 2.4). In manufacturing industry, employment fell dramatically by 1¾ million between 1979 and 1985. Even the service sector contracted between 1979 and 1983 before rising again. In 1955 40 per cent of employment was in the nation's manufacturing industry. By 1987 this had halved to just 20 per cent. By contrast, services such as transport, distribution and finance have seen their share of total employment rise from 45 per cent to 70 per cent over that thirty-year period. From 1979 to 1986 manufacturing employment fell from over 7 million to 5.2 million.

Table 2.4: Employees in employment, UK

Industry	1971 (000s)	1976 (000s)	1985 (000s)
Agriculture, forestry, fishing	432	393	338
Metals, engineering, vehicles	3,705	3,330	2,612
Energy, water supply	797	721	613
Extraction, chemicals	1,278	1,157	799
Other manufacturing	3,102	2,794	2,122
Construction	1,207	1,252	970
Distribution, hotels, catering	3,678	3,964	4,470
Transport, communications	1,550	1,456	1,304
Banking, financial services	1,336	1,494	1,972
Other services	5,036	5,975	6,266
All industries and services	22,122	22,543[a]	21,467

Note: a. Includes 8700 employees not in individual industry group.

Source: *Social Trends*, 17

Another important change that has taken place concerns the rise of the part-timer. In 1951 there were just 800,000 part-time workers; but in the last decade the number of part-time employees has increased by over a million and now stands at 5 million. Part-time employees were 21 per cent of all employees in 1981 and over 23 per cent in 1986. Forecasts from the Institute of Employment Research (IER) now expect this to rise to 28 per cent by 1995. Today 85 per cent of these part-time employees are women. Other than the massive increase in unemployment experienced in the early 1980s, probably the most dramatic change that has taken place in the labour market in the post-1945 period concerns the number and proportion of women who are active in the economy. It is now expected that by 1991 one-half of women aged 16 and over will be economically active (the female economic activity rate is the proportion of women who are in the civilian labour force). In 1971 the figure was 43 per cent.

This trend towards the increasing participation of women is part of the longer-term trend for married women, especially, to look for and to gain employment. One in five married women is now in full-time work: a further quarter work part-time. Women's employment is concentrated in the services sector, in particular in hotels, catering, distribution, public services, finance and other services, but not in transport and communication. The industries which employ a high proportion of women are mainly those that have expanded employment, particularly part-time employment, since the early 1970s. Many employers in the services sector continue to search out part-time employees to fill their vacancies, sometimes splitting up a full-time post in so doing.

In 1986 just over one in five employees were in professional-type jobs, just under one in five was an unskilled worker, such as labourer or operative, and 18 per cent were in sales or personal services (see Figure 2.3). According to the IER the share of these occupational groups in total employment is likely to change somewhat in the years to 1995. We can expect a higher proportion of managers and professionals and a continuing drop in the proportion of employees earning their living from unskilled and semi-skilled 'blue collar' work. Opportunities for those with low-level or no skills and qualifications will continue to diminish in the 1990s. This is in part a reflection of just what is going to be happening to the main economic sectors, such as manufacturing, primary industries and the services (see below).

VACANCIES

In Great Britain official statistics on job vacancies are collated and published by the Department of Employment. It is estimated that

Figure 2.3: Percentage shares in total employment 1986 and 1995 of the main occupational groups

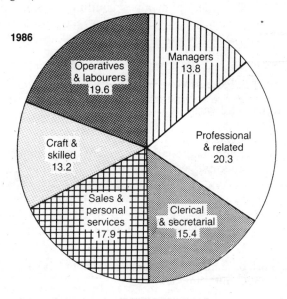

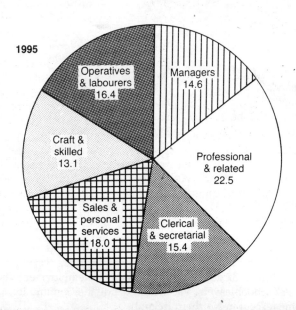

Source: Institute of Employment Research, Warwick University, 1987.

these vacancy statistics represent only about one-third of all the vacancies that might exist at any one time. Jobs are filled by employers using a variety of means, including agencies, advertisements in the press or specialist journals, through existing employees or through unsolicited letters of enquiry. The official vacancy count mainly comprises those jobs on offer that are notified to Jobcentres, the Careers Service or the more specialist agency, Professional and Executive Recruitment (PER). There is, of course, no compulsion for employing organisations to use any of these facilities to fill vacancies.

Information on vacancies allows us to lay to rest for good the popular misconception that seems especially prevalent in parts of the south of England, namely that there are sufficient job vacancies around for the unemployed if only they had a bit more motivation and transport. In August 1985, when unemployment stood at over 3.2 million, the number of job vacancies nationally stood at just 179,000, according to the official vacancy statistics. Even if we err on the side of overestimating the total number of jobs available by

Table 2.5: Stock of unfilled vacancies as notified to Jobcentres and the Unemployment Count[a], June 1987

Region	Vacancies (V)	Unemployment (U)	Ratio of U to V (U/V)
South-east	86,800	669,400	7.7
East Anglia	7,900	71,300	9.0
South-west	20,800	169,700	8.2
West Midlands	20,800	303,300	14.6
East Midlands	12,700	181,600	14.3
Yorkshire and Humberside	15,800	282,900	17.9
North-west	24,600	398,900	16.2
North	12,000	210,800	17.6
Wales	11,700	151,500	12.9
Scotland	18,300	340,300	18.6
Great Britain	231,300	2,779,800	12.0
Northern Ireland	2,000	125,600	62.8
United Kingdom	233,300	2,905,300	12.5

Note: a. On June 1987 definitions of registered unemployment: the figures exclude 1987 school-leavers. Vacancies exclude the Community Programme (except in Northern Ireland).
Source: *Employment Gazette.*

rounding this up to 200,000 and then multiplying by three, this still only gives a maximum 600,000 spaces for the 3.2 million registered unemployed to fit into in 1985. In June 1987, when great claims were being made for falling unemployment and rising vacancies, as can be seen from Table 2.5, registered unemployment stood at 2.9 million, whereas notified vacancies amounted to just 233,300 giving a ratio of official jobless to vacancies of over 12 to 1. Taking into account un-notified job vacancies this would provide only 700,000 vacancies nationwide. And even if the vacancies were regionally distributed to fit the location of the unemployed, and even if the unemployed had all the right attributes in terms of skills and qualifications to meet employers' requirements (and they do not), then you would still have over 2 million officially jobless people to place. There has always been a mismatch between the unemployed and vacancies—by industry, by occupation and by region. But even if there were not, the numerical differences now are just so great that it is ludicrous to suggest that jobs are there for the taking if only the unemployed were to get on their bikes and look for work.

Vacancy information also permits a comparison to be made of the relative chances of the unemployed finding work on a regional or industrial basis. Table 2.5 gives details of the stock of unfilled vacancies in June 1987. It also provides the unemployment total by region. We can use this information to calculate what are called U/V ratios, simply by dividing the unemployment count number by the number of vacancies in each region. This U/V figure can tell us about the ratio of unemployed people to official vacancies in different parts of the country, to all vacancies (by dividing the U/V figure again by three) and how the situation is changing over time, if we were to repeat the exercise for a number of months or years. What Table 2.5 reveals is the massive difference in the chances of the unemployed finding a job according to where they live. The exercise can also be repeated for more local areas. The reader is invited to get hold of the *Employment Gazette* (published monthly by the Department of Employment) and to carry out this exercise for his or her own town or country. There is nothing like it for disabusing oneself about the number of jobs around to meet the needs of the unemployed in any particular area. The further mismatch in terms of skill, occupation and industrial background just serves to make the situation much, much worse than the regional figures imply.

JOBS FOR THE FUTURE?

The labour force is still growing: from 1984 to 1987 this growth has averaged about 120,000 a year. Population change has accounted for 100,000 of this, and an extra 20,000 or so is coming from re-entrants to the labour force, especially women. The labour force is expected to continue to grow until 1990 before tailing off somewhat as smaller age-groups join the labour force. For the remainder of the 1980s, then, new jobs at the rate of at least 100,000 or so a year have to be found for unemployment just to stand still. Supporters of existing employment policies point to recent 'successes' in job-creation, and consider that absorbing these extra numbers as well as making some dent in the unemployment total may not be too difficult. One particular claimed success was the creation of 480,000 jobs in the eighteen months to autumn 1984. These jobs comprised an increase of 318,000 in the self-employed, 5000 in the armed forces and just 157,000 additional employees in employment. But this increase of 480,000 has to be seen in the context of the loss of 2 million jobs in the eighteen months to March 1983. Not that impressive a record!

So where is it expected that the new jobs will be coming from? A disproportionate amount of time is being spent on talking-up the prospects in a number of sectors, the most important of which are probably tourism services (and other services more generally), electronics and the information technology sector, and self-employment.

Certainly, self-employment has been growing and now stands at over 2½ million people. The self-employed numbers have been fuelled in the 1980s by the financial assistance of the Enterprise Allowance Scheme, which pays unemployed people £40 a week for a year to set up their own businesses (see Chapter 7). Of course, those claiming such an allowance are no longer included among the unemployed. Self-employment was also given a boost by the very high numbers of people becoming unemployed with some redundancy pay in the earlier 1980s. In comparison with the job losses that have occurred in manufacturing, the rise in self-employment alone can do little to eat into the unemployment total.

As noted above, the number of part-time jobs has increased by over a million in the last decade. Many of these jobs have been in tourism, hotel and catering. It is estimated that between 1.1 million and 1.4 million people now earn their living working in tourism. Between December 1984 and December 1985 employment in tourism-related services grew by 43,000. Of these jobs 8,000 went to men and 25,000 to women (18,000 of these part-time). Certainly, tourism and leisure is growing as an employer, but many of these jobs are low paid, part-time and seasonal. Employees are working in a sector of the economy that is notorious for its poor pay and working conditions, its lack of unionisation, and the often temporary nature of the jobs available. The demand here is only for a certain kind of labour. The jobs being created in the leisure trade (and there is little doubt that this is a trend that will continue) are no good substitute for all the 'male' full-time jobs that have been lost since 1979.

So much for tourism, but what of that particular sector of the economy which is supposed to have such a sexy and glamorous image—electronics? The number of people *directly* employed in electronics in the United Kingdom is actually *lower* now than it was in the late 1970s. In the six years to 1984, 60,000 people lost their jobs in electronics, and at just over 300,000 electronics employs in total fewer people than the number who have lost their jobs in the textile industry since the mid-1970s. It is true that smaller, more specialist businesses have been springing up in electronics. The biggest employers, however, have shed thousands of jobs in the 1980s, all having reduced their staffing. Electronics is just not the huge jobs machine that it is sometimes painted.

These two areas, then, tourism and electronics, where the general but poorly informed view is that they can greatly assist the crisis of unemployment, are unlikely to deliver. Electronics has been declining, and while tourism and leisure have grown, the demand has been, is, and will be only for certain types of labour. They are not the answer.

Forecasting employment and unemployment levels for the future is an exercise fraught with difficulties. One of the most authoritative forecasts of future employment has come from the Institute of Manpower Studies, based at Sussex University. According to a 1986 report published by the Institute, the number of employees in the productive industries, such as manufacturing and construction, is expected to fall by a further 665,000 up to 1990. An additional 150,000 jobs will be lost from some services, such as transport and public services (Figure 2.4). The number of employees in other services such as leisure, recreation, finance and business services is expected to increase by just over 400,000 in compensation. The balance of this forecast, then, is that Britain's employed labour force is expected to fall by an additional 400,000 up to 1990. For the UK as a whole, and including an assessment of the growth of self-employment during this period, there will be a net loss of 125,000 in the workforce.

If we set this against an additional 100,000 people entering the labour market each year, then on present trends there can be no real easing of the unemployment problem. Indeed, on existing trends there is the probability that it will get worse. According the IER's 1987 annual review, the stimulus to jobs resulting from UK economic growth will only result in registered unemployment falling to 2.8 million by 1990 and 2.5 million by 1995. (At the time of writing even the Confederation of British industry are expecting unemployment to stop falling in mid-1988 before starting to rise again!) The IER anticipates that *employment* overall will rise at about 0.5 per cent per year, with most growth being in part-time

31

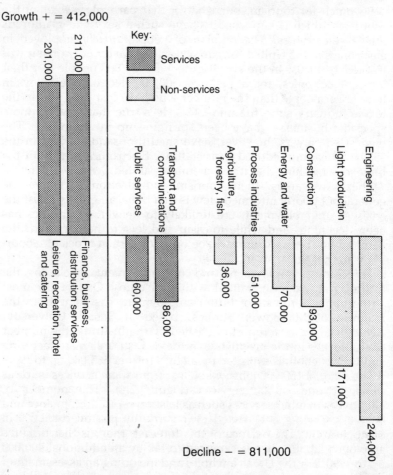

Figure 2.4: The growth and decline of employees in employment in Great Britain, 1985–90

Growth + = 412,000

Key:
- Services
- Non-services

201,000 — Leisure, recreation, hotel and catering
211,000 — Finance, business, distribution services

60,000 — Public services
86,000 — Transport and communications
36,000 — Agriculture, forestry, fish
51,000 — Process industries
70,000 — Energy and water
93,000 — Construction
171,000 — Light production
244,000 — Engineering

Decline − = 811,000

Source: Rajan and Pearson, *UK Occupation and Employment Trends to 1990*, Institute of Manpower Studies.

employees, especially women. Manufacturing is expected to continue with job losses, at a rate of some 1 per cent a year, 500,000 jobs in all. Since 1975 jobs in manufacturing have perished at 3 per cent a year. The compensating job gains come in construction, distribution and transport, hotels and catering and business and other services and in public services such as education and health care.

The Organisation of Economic Co-operation and Development

(OECD) have estimated that employment in the UK must grow by at least 1 per cent a year every year just to hold steady the numbers unemployed or on special schemes. Without a radical rethink of the priorities of government the prospects for 1990 and beyond look bleak. As in *The Hitchhiker's Guide to the Galaxy* by Douglas Adams, there is a limit to the number of us who can become self-employed by opening shoe shops!

CONCLUSIONS

Those decades when unemployment stayed at 6 per cent or less are, for many, just a fond memory. Those decades, and the policies pursued and the consensus over objectives, are now frequently rubbished by the Conservative government and its supporters. They regard the full-employment years as years of feather-bedding, years that handed too much power to employees and employee-representative organisations. They do not believe in the North–South divide. They have scant respect for, or any experience of, manufacturing industry. Pushing registered unemployment to over 3 million, and the real level of unemployment much higher, is regarded as a low price to pay for the adoption of a new sense of realism in the labour market and, it is argued, for keeping inflation low. (In passing, it is worth pointing out that with the commodity-price trends of the 1980s, only a really incompetent and perverse government could have kept inflation at double figures during this time.)

So, the full-employment 'good times' were not really good times at all, runs the Tebbit-speak of the 1980s. The 'bad times' of mass unemployment are not so bad, according to Lord Young. And new jobs are coming, just around the currently painful corner. It is clear, however, as we have seen, that on existing policies for the unemployed, the 'good times' have been followed by the 'bad times'. In the 1990s all that is in prospect are more 'bad times'.

3. Why Has Unemployment Risen?

In Chapter 2 we saw how unemployment in the 1950s and up to the mid-1960s was at a lower rate than even Beveridge and Keynes considered possible, dipping as low as just over 1 per cent in the mid-1950s. Throughout this period, then, unemployment averaged less than 2 per cent. In the mid- and later 1960s unemployment was kept below 4 per cent, rising to about that level in the recession of the early 1970s. It is interesting to note in passing the horror with which the prospect of 1 million unemployed was greeted at the beginning of the 1970s. In 1975–8 unemployment was over 6 per cent, dropping back somewhat in 1978–9 before increasing three-fold since 1979.

A ratchet effect has been experienced since the 1970–2 recession, with unemployment in the upturn following recession being higher than in the previous upturn in the economic cycle. At the peaks and troughs employment has been successively lower and unemployment successively higher than in earlier cycles.

The pattern of unemployment that has to be explained, then, is of rather slowly and erratically rising unemployment from the mid-1960s to the late 1970s, and of a massive increase in unemployment immediately following the election of a Conservative government in 1979. Certainly, there is good reason to think that the factors affecting unemployment changed in relative importance in the 1979 to 1987 period. And if it is possible to satisfactorily and

accurately identify the causes of our current high level of unemployment, then this should offer more than a little guidance
to the ways unemployment can be dramatically reduced. Is it really
so much more difficult to put 2 million people back to work in three
years than to create an additional 2 million unemployed in the
same period?

Economists have three conventional and traditional explanations
for unemployment and carefully distinguish them. These are
frictional, cyclical and structural unemployment. Frictional
unemployment will always exist on some scale. There are always
job-changers who leave one job and at any point in time will be
looking for another. In addition, there are entrants to the labour
market such as school- and college-leavers or married-women
returners seeking their first job or a job after a career break. And
even in times of 'full employment' some people will be hard to
place in work and for one reason and another find it extremely
difficult to find employment. Frictional unemployment can be
considered as the minimum level of unemployment below which a
labour market just cannot go. As noted in Chapter 2, for the UK
this level of full employment was thought to be attained at 3 per
cent unemployment, or an unemployment level at about 800,000 in
the late 1980s. The UK's experience with 1 and 2 per cent
unemployment in the 1950s led to a downward revision in the
potential scale of frictional unemployment.

The notion of structural unemployment is an important one. It
results from an imbalance between the labour force available for
work and the demands by employing organisations for certain
types of labour. People available for work vary, of course, in terms
of their age, their skills and qualifications, gender, where they live
and their mobility and so on. The productive structure of all
economies changes over time, with new skills in demand, old
industries declining and new ones growing, and the geographical
location of the old and the new changing, albeit rather slowly.
Structural unemployment can result from a mismatch of skills in
demand and those in supply, the speed with which the productive
structure is changing, and lags in the labour market's ability to
adapt or a shortage of the right kind of investment. There is also, of
course, a regional dimension.

Cyclical unemployment, the third type, can be considered as the
extent to which the actual level of unemployment exceeds frictional
unemployment at a time when the productive structure is not
creating special unemployment difficulties. If the labour force is in
tune with or is well-adapted to the structure of the economy (in
terms of skills, location and so on), then the excess of actual
unemployment over the frictional minimum represents the cyclical
element in total unemployment. References are often made in the
economics literature to the tendency for the economy to move

successively through cycles of upturn and recession, boom and trough. With structural effects remaining roughly the same, cyclical unemployment is the difference in unemployment rate between that experienced at the top of the upturn and that apparent in the depths of recession.

These three concepts of unemployment are quite useful in looking at the UK's pattern of unemployment in the years since 1945. In a year such as 1977, for example, attempts can be made to split off frictional, structural and cyclical unemployment, and to pursue policy initiatives that can aim at, for example, reducing the length of job-search for the newly unemployed or for school-leavers (frictional) or going for crash retraining programmes or mobility assistance (structural). These concepts, however real, present only part of the picture when examining the causes of unemployment increase.

When examining why the UK's rate of growth was lower than our major industrial competitors, Nicholas Kaldor coined the phrase 'premature maturity'. The hypothesis was advanced that the UK, as the first country to experience the modern industrial revolution, had reached a state of maturity before its full industrial potential had been realised. This is related to the deindustrialisation thesis put forward by others. Deindustrialisation refers to the tendency for industrial output (and especially employment) to plateau, then fall, but without the workers who are displaced, especially from manufacturing, successfully gaining employment elsewhere. The reasons advanced for this deindustrialisation are manifold, but include a tendency for manufacturing to become more capital intensive, particularly with investment in new, labour-saving technology. The rapid industrialisation of other countries, especially in South East Asia, might exacerbate the deindustrialisation trend.

A loss of employment in the industrial sector due to capital investment may partly reflect the kind of investment that has been taking place, particularly when UK companies attempt to compete at home and abroad with low-wage, long-hour companies abroad. Much of the investment that has taken place has been of the labour-saving rather than labour-using kind. Labour-saving investment can have a marked effect on indicators of labour productivity, with more being produced in terms on both volume and value, with the same number of employees, or with similar amounts being produced with far fewer employees. Displaced workers might expect to find alternative employment with other companies or in public-service occupations. Expenditure cuts and planned manpower reductions in the public sector in the 1980s have shut off this latter route.

With investment in labour-saving technology in manufacturing especially, output per person or per man-hour will increase.

Certainly, in the 1970s much was being made of the low levels of productivity in much of UK industry in comparison with international competitors. This poor competitive position has been held partly responsible by many for the increase in unemployment. However, some of the cruder productivity measures often used take little account of the capital with which labour has to work, and international differences in investment. Output-per-man-hour kinds of measure mean little unless they are also closely related to capital equipment. Certainly, since 1980 there have been substantial productivity gains in British industry (although manufacturing output until the autumn of 1987 was still *lower* than in 1979!). This can mainly be explained by the fact that the least productive and most marginal companies, and the least productive plant elsewhere, have closed down in the 1980s, thus boosting dramatically the average productivity levels.

The shake-out of employment in manufacturing, which accounts for most of the jobs lost since 1979, has been accompanied by a changed perspective on public-sector employment, whether industrial or service. Particularly influential was the Bacon and Eltis book in the 1970s, *Britain's Economic Problem: Too Few Producers*, which argued that the market or productive sectors of the economy were being deprived of manpower, finance and resources generally by the burgeoning growth of the non-market sector. The rate of growth of employment in the public services was considered excessive, and the public services' appetites were 'crowding out' the productive or market employers to the detriment of the British economy. Since 1979 public-sector employment opportunities have declined sharply. With such restrictive manpower policies being adopted in the public sector, and with the private-sector services employers unable to take up the slack of displaced manufacturing employees, a structural mismatch occurred in the early 1980s. This imbalance or mismatch has been greatly worsened by government anti-inflation policies.

Two other reasons advanced for the rise in unemployment which will be developed below, concern the wages and salaries of employees and the power and influence of trade unions. These are thought to be connected by economists who place a special emphasis on the effects of these two factors. The 'excessive' growth of wages without a corresponding advance in productivity, it is argued, has led, in common parlance, to employees pricing themselves out of jobs. Companies have been encouraged to reduce their headcount and to invest in labour-saving machinery by the rising price of labour. Trade unions, by representing their members in wage negotiations, are held to bear a heavy responsibility for this state of affairs. Union restrictive practices, in particular demarcation, overmanning, closed shops and the ready pursuit of industrial action, are considered by some to have been a direct cause of high unemployment.

Now this discussion of the causes of the present crisis of unemployment is interesting enough. But it does not help us to identify the *relative importance* of the different factors that have led to high unemployment. There are a number of pieces of research by economists that do attempt such a systematic scrutiny of the causes of unemployment. It is, however, sometimes difficult to get economists to agree on causes, let alone on cures. In this chapter, and later on, two contrasting schools of thought will be presented and discussed. These schools of thought differ fundamentally in the way they interpret the workings of the economy, in their analysis of the causes of unemployment and, rather naturally, in the policy measures they propose to alleviate the situation. I will attempt to be fair to both, but I find myself more convinced by the evidence of one group than the other. The first set of economic evidence on causes comes from the neo-Keynesians, who are persuaded of the importance and benign influence of government intervention in the workings of the economy.

NEO-KEYNESIAN CAUSES

Richard Layard and Stephen Nickell have attempted to estimate the causes of unemployment in the UK for the period 1956 to 1983. Their method is rather complex and statistically difficult for the non-economist, but their findings are of great importance. Central to their method is the creation of a model that seeks to explain changes in male unemployment. Using a statistical technique called regression analysis, they then try to calculate the relative importance of the different factors thought to affect unemployment. A simplified version of their model of the causes of unemployment would look something like this:

$$UN = \int (t, b, u, p, mm, d, y)$$

This is not complicated. It is not even mathematics (yet). It is just economists' shorthand for writing that the change in the male unemployment rate (UN) is a function of ($\int$) or caused by a range of influences, including employers' labour taxes such as national insurance (t); the extent to which unemployment benefits replace earnings while at work (b) (see also Chapter 5); union militancy or the power of trade unions as measured by their ability to get higher wages for their members in comparison with non-trade unionists doing similar jobs (u); real import prices (p); the mismatch in the labour market as reflected in any imbalance in the pattern of vacancies in comparison with the skills of the unemployed (mm); the aggregate demand in the economy (d); and the imposition or otherwise of some kind of incomes policy (y).

What we have then is a hypothesis that changes in male unemployment are affected by these different factors. This works quite well for each of the three time periods considered within 1956 to 1983. Until 1979 changes in unemployment were dominated by employers' labour taxes, a closer relationship between benefits and earnings (benefit-replacement ratios) and a rise in union power. The amount of demand in the economy played a part too.

In the latest period considered, 1975–9 to 1980–3, when male unemployment in the UK trebled, the unemployment rate increasing by 7 per cent, one factor alone stands out as causing the increase. The model explains 6.59 per cent of the 7 per cent unemployment-rate increase. Within this, the factor that explains nearly four-fifths of the rise in unemployment is aggregate demand. So, according to Layard and Nickell, it has been a gross deficiency in demand in the economy that accounts for the bulk of the increase in unemployment since the late 1970s. But just what is this rather nebulous aggregate demand?

Aggregate demand has a number of constituent elements, including:

- spending by individuals on consumption
- public spending on goods and services
- private investment
- the excess of exports over imports

So, a deficiency in these elements that comprise aggregate demand can be held accountable, according to Layard and Nickell (and others) for the largest part of the increase in unemployment that has occurred since the late 1970s. The implications of this for formulating policies to get Britain back to work are considered in detail in Chapters 8 and 9. For the time being it is worth noting how policies to reduce (rather than increase) public spending will make matters worse, how policies that increase the amount of income taken from individuals or companies through taxation will make matters worse, how the failure to try to maintain the spending levels of those who become unemployed and thus keeping their consumption high, will also make matters worse. With the onset of high unemployment consumer spending, by definition, will drop. It also creates a separate economic problem of its own—£20 billion a year is currently being spent in paying benefits to the unemployed, and in foregoing the income tax and national insurance they would be paying if at work.

In the 1980s neo-Keynesian economists have argued powerfully with statistical support, that it is a chronic shortage of demand in the UK, and in many other countries, that has led to the unprecedentedly rapid increase in unemployment to unprecedented heights. Layard and Nickell, as noted above, estimate that deficiency in demand explains 80 per cent of the rise in unemployment. Hughes and Perlman, in 1986, estimated that 70 per cent of UK unemployment and 40–50 per cent of unemployment in the USA was due to a shortage in aggregate demand.

Government policies, with their emphasis on tackling the spectre of inflation, certainly made matters much worse from 1979 to 1983. Anti-inflationary policies, such as maintaining a very high value of sterling which kept imported goods very cheap while destroying manufacturing exports, and adopting a high-interest rate stance, created much of the unemployment that ministers now apparently lament. But the greatest policy failure was a policy omission. Intervention to correct the chronic shortage of demand was ruled out in favour of the adoption of a different set of supply-side or monetarist policies. Patrick Minford of Liverpool University is just one of a number of supply-siders whose views have been sympathetically received by the Thatcher government.

NEO-CLASSICAL CAUSES

Economists now sheltering under the neo-classical school of thought have their feet firmly placed in nineteenth-century notions of how markets work, including the labour market. They perceive the role of government as simply to ensure, as nearly as possible, that markets operate smoothly. So, if there is unemployment this is an indication that the supply of labour (people looking for work) exceeds the demand for labour (employers offering jobs). Given that labour, like any other commodity or service, has a price, its wage or salary, if there is an excess of supply over demand that price should fall. There will be a wage level which ensures that all those who want work will find it. The continued existence of unemployment is an indication then, that a range of factors are likely to be in existence that impede the operation of the labour market. Much of the research work of these economists has focused on identifying these inhibiting factors, gauging their relative sizes, and making policy recommendations aimed at removing the identified problems in the working of the labour market. Patrick Minford is probably the foremost exponent of this approach in the UK.

The Minford analysis used some 1300 factors in attempting to unravel the causes of unemployment and its possible remedies. As with the Layard and Nickell exercise for the non-economist, the method used is extremely complicated. Patrick Minford's book *Unemployment: Cause and Cure*, together with a number of journal articles, summarise the conclusions of this work. In short, Minford identifies what are believed to be the 'two major distortions in the UK labour market'. The first, and most important, of these is the benefits system for the unemployed. The second culpable factor is the power of the trade unions. With fundamental changes to welfare benefits and trade unions Minford is convinced that a long-run fall in unemployment of 1.7 million can be achieved. (Keynes, of course, considered that in the long run we are all dead!)

But in what ways are benefits and unions so important? Dealing first with benefits, Minford is convinced that 'the fundamental cause of unemployment is the operation of the unemployment benefit system'. Since an unemployed person can claim benefit indefinitely (unemployment benefit, possibly with top-up for the first year if eligible, and supplementary benefit and its replacement thereafter) there is no incentive for him or her to return to work quickly, or to return for a wage which after tax, national insurance work expenses and then some, pays little more than the benefit entitlement. Minford argues that the operation of the unemployment benefits system represents, in effect, a floor below which wages cannot go. The ability of wages to act as a flexible price of labour in times of labour surplus is therefore greatly inhibited. Following from this, reforms of the benefit system are proposed. The main proposal is that in future benefits paid should not exceed 70 per cent of previous take-home pay. Minford estimates that such a measure would reduce the unemployment total by about 750,000 over a four-year period. In effect, what is suggested is a cut in the real value of benefits to the unemployed. Given the extent of poverty already among those losing their jobs and their families, and the *fact* (see Chapter 5) that only a small proportion of the unemployed receive in benefits anything close to their previous earnings, the clear impact of such a measure would be even greater hardship for those out of work. There is also enshrined in this proposal the tacit belief that much unemployment is voluntary, something that a cursory comparison of the unemployment and vacancy statistics should dispel. Minford also has proposals on eligibility for benefits which would mean in future that no choice would be involved in claiming benefits or 'earning'. The creation of a jobs pool is proposed (which could involve an expansion of something like the Community Programme). For those aged under 25, benefits would be available and conditional upon the claimant accepting a pool 'job' within three months. For the older unemployed, benefit would be stopped after six months. This is just a variant on the US workfare scheme which requires the unemployed to 'earn' their benefit. The eligibility rules on benefit would also be tightened up.

On trade unions, the problem is perceived as being the way unions can raise their members' wages relative to non-Union members. The union jobs, then, are the most highly sought after, but are in short supply. Alternative work in the more poorly rewarded non-union sector are insufficient to mop up all those looking for work because the benefit system keeps these wages unrealistically and unacceptably high. Union power, it is argued, has to be first contained and then dissipated. Only by taking action against the restrictive practices of the unions can the labour market operate more nearly to a free market in labour, with supply and demand determining price (wages), and with the reformed benefit system just acting as a lower-level safety net. Firm legislation is proposed by Minford and his associates to further dilute the influence of the unions.

Other actions on wages and conditions of employment are proposed. A number of employee groups and industries are affected by Wages Councils and wage regulations. These set minimum wages to be paid to certain employees at particular levels. They are concentrated in the worst-paying and often least secure sectors of the economy. Minford proposes their abolition. Lower wages for employees in these sectors are likely to result (especially for young people). It is held that Wages Councils have assisted in pricing people out of work and that an expansion of employment would result from their abolition. In fact Wages Council operations peaked in 1953 (when unemployment was 2 per cent), covering 3.5 million workers within the network of 66 Councils. There are still over 20 Wages Councils covering some 2.5 million employees, the largest group being those working in the hotel and catering industry with over 500,000 employees. Over 10 per cent of the labour force are still covered by Wages Councils. For Minford and Conservative government ministers, Wages Councils are a symbol of the inflexible labour market. The Low Pay Unit have made estimates of the affects of abolition. The pay of those currently covered would fall by 2.5 per cent on average: remember these are some of the lowest-paid workers in the British economy. An estimated additional 70,000 jobs would result from abolition, but a high proportion of these jobs, given their part-time nature, would not be filled by the registered unemployed. Work by the Department of Employment on the earlier abolition of other Wages Councils detected little increase in the number of jobs available.

In addition to action on wages and Wages Councils, employment protection and health and safety legislation should be watered down, according to Minford. The qualifying period for enjoying the benefits of the Employment Protection Act should be raised to five years, instead of the current one year for employees, but two years for those in smaller companies. Small businesses should be exempted from all employment protection for their employees. Health and Safety rules should become advisory with self-regulation the order of the day. As far as other employment laws are concerned, Minford argues that 'benign neglect should be shown by the executive arm of the state'.

The neo-classical supply-siders, then, look forward in eager anticipation, to the day when the UK is a hire-and-fire, insecure, employer-dominated operation, unfettered by organised labour, welfare-benefit protection for the unemployed or wage control for its most vulnerable employees. The influence of these views on the Thatcher-led governments in power since 1979 is discussed at the end of the chapter. Their pervasive effects in the 1980s and for the future should not be underestimated.

THE GOVERNMENT VIEW OF CAUSES

Unemployment rises when we move too slowly to meet new customer needs, overseas competition and technological change, and when pay and prices—the link between supply and demand—adjust too slowly. There is no basic lack of demand; the reason we cannot use our full labour force is that we have not yet adapted well enough, particularly in our job market, to be able to exploit it.

This quote is taken from the 1985 White Paper, *Employment: The Challenge for the Nation*. In it, the government sets out information on the failings of the economy in the past (which it is putting to rights), details of the labour force and the labour market (which is failing the economy but getting better) and a 'programme' for the future. Great play is made of the achievements of the economy in the 1979–85 period, albeit with over 3 million people unemployed, and laments the fact that such progress had not been accompanied by lower unemployment. The government interpretation of the causes of unemployment is at great odds with those neo-Keynesian economists such as Layard and Nickell, who have pointed to a chronic deficiency of demand as the main cause. The government even denies the link between its own anti-inflation policies and the rising tide of unemployment. This link is now even accepted by those economists favourably disposed towards many of the Conservative government's policies for the labour market. Minford accepts that, 'Part of the current higher unemployment rate is the effect associated with the Conservative Government's policies to reduce inflation in the UK'.

If it is not its own policies, just how does the government explain the increase in unemployment and its continuation at high levels? The world recession clearly has played a part, this is accepted by all. But the fact that UK unemployment rose more quickly and to higher levels *earlier* than most other industrialised countries still needs explaining. The government is clearest on what has *not* caused high unemployment:

43

ck of demand.

ck of public sector investment.

chnological change.

cher government maintains that demand has been
, and that employment would be higher if so much
demand had not been spirited away in the form of higher pay for
those in work and higher prices for all. There is reiteration that
inflation is a major cause of high unemployment. On public-sector
investments, the view is maintained *not* that such investment has
been sufficient, but that public-sector capital spending does not
rate well as a means of creating jobs. No mention is made that such
spending is *investment* in infrastructure for the future with a use-
life that can be measured in decades. Whether £26,000 per job
created on public infrastructure investment in education or £16,000
per job in housing is too expensive, is a judgement (see Chapter 8).
Certainly, in comparison with income tax cuts which create one job
(through extra consumer spending) for every £47,000 given away
by the Chancellor of the Exchequer, public investment looks rather
a bargain for both the government and, especially so, for the
unemployed.

Technological change is a factor often referred to as being a
potential and possible cause of unemployment. The scare estimates from the 1960s and 1970s of massive technological
unemployment have yet to be even nearly achieved. Layard and
Nickell were agnostic on the possibility of some unemployment
being caused by the development, introduction and extended use
of new technology of different kinds. Kevin Hawkins has
expressed some concern about the balance of capital investment
being a contributory cause—in particular the emphasis on labour-
saving rather than labour-using capital as the relative prices of
labour and capital changed during the 1970s. The government
believes that, overall, new technology leads to the creation of more
rather than fewer jobs, as demand is created for new products with
new modes of production. Certainly, there is some evidence for
this view, provided that structural mismatches (particularly in
labour skills and mobility) can be overcome, and that new technology has a domestic base when it comes to research, development, manufacture and assembly.

So, the government has clearly defined views on what has *not*
caused unemployment. It is the operations of the labour market
that are held mainly responsible for prevailing levels of unemployment. As *Employment: The Challenge for the Nation* asserts: 'The
biggest single cause of our high unemployment is the failure of our
jobs market, the weak link in our economy'. In this single sentence
the Thatcher government has nailed its colours and its policies
firmly to the supply-sider, neo-classical mast of the labour
economists' ketch. What follows then becomes predictable.

With an excess supply of labour of over 3 million, the argument proferred is that the market for labour is not working well. Thus the analysis suggests ways for improving the labour market by improving and changing the supply of labour (the demand side is left untainted by government intervention). Labour needed to be improved in quality, needed to be better trained. Labour had to be 'improved' in terms of cost, i.e. made cheaper. Labour supply had to be improved in terms of incentives, especially incentives to work. The implication of this is that the differential between benefits and wages should be widened. While some action could be taken on increasing net pay through income tax cuts (in the 1980s eaten up by that other tax on income—national insurance) clearly it is action on benefits that is mainly anticipated. Trade unions are also held responsible for the lack of improvement in pay, with labour just not cheap enough. The government complain that labour is not flexible enough. Trade union resistance is again held largely responsible here. In addition, the labour market has to be improved in terms of 'freedom'. This is Tebbit-speak for substantially reducing the employment protection offered workers in law.

If a comparison is made between the Thatcher government's analysis of the causes of the UK's high unemployment and its general remedies, and those causes offered rather more thoughtfully by Richard Layard and Stephen Nickell on the one hand, and Patrick Minford and associates on the other, you do not need to have qualifications from the London Business School to work out just where there is most accord. Clearly, it is the neo-classical/monetarist/supply-sider argument that holds sway in the UK governments of the 1980s. There are clear parallels between many of the academic supply-sider proposals put forward in the late 1970s and the 1980s and the changes enacted by government. The politicians in implementation may have taken a softer line of risk-aversion than that rumbustiously argued by the neo-classical economists (who, of course, will not be held to account by any electorate), but the parallels are there.

THE GOVERNMENT RESPONSE

Those who argue that the government has no coherent strategy or policy for the labour market or for unemployment are misguided. The package is a carefully worked out one, that is not being implemented in a hurry, rather to the impatience of some supply-siders. Let us consider just what forms these actions have taken and are taking.

(1)Action has taken place on wages in a number of ways. Many

Wages Councils have been abolished: more will go. The allowances paid to the unemployed participating on government special schemes (see Chapter 7) such as the YTS or the Community Programme are deliberately kept very low. This is partly to increase incentives to get (back) into 'proper' employment, and partly to lower wage expectations in anticipation that individuals on such schemes will now lower their sights and accept low-wage jobs. Subsidies to employers to take on new workers provided that they pay low wages reinforces this. Greater emphasis is now being placed on the 'reservation wage' of the unemployed when attending for interviews at Unemployment Benefit Offices: an unrealistically high assessment of the minimum acceptable wage in work is grounds for stopping benefit.

(2) Further action has been and is being taken on benefits. Since 1979 unemployment benefit has become liable to income tax. Earnings-related unemployment benefit has been abandoned. Tests of availability for work have been tightened up. Benefit levels have dismally failed to keep up with earnings, and according to some statistics have not even kept pace with the increase in prices. In early 1987 new rules were introduced which mean that the home-owning unemployed now only have one-half of the interest on their mortgages paid for them for the first four months of unemployment. Prior to this all interest repayments (but not capital) were paid on supplementary benefit. This change will save the relatively insignificant amount of £23 million, and affects 75,000 families. Legislation is planned to ensure that young people turning down the offer of a YTS place will be refused any benefit. Prior to this they had to wait until the September after leaving school before being able to claim any benefit. A similar rule may well be enacted for other groups of unemployed people if and when there are sufficient places on the Community Programme and the Job Training Scheme to cater for all those eligible. This is 'workfare'. From April 1988, it becomes necessary to have made national insurance contributions for two years in order to claim unemployment benefit. This would double the requirement, and 350,000 claimants of unemployment and sickness benefit will become ineligible.

(3) Action on labour 'discipline' has been enacted and more is planned. The qualifying period for protection against unfair dismissal has been extended from six months to one year generally, but to two years in companies with 20 or fewer workers. The employment protection rights of part-time workers have been substantially diluted. More changes are planned, particularly affecting women employees. Until 1987 if someone left a job voluntarily and 'without just cause' they could be subjected to six weeks' loss of benefit, and usually

were. This penalty for leaving a job has now been increased to 13 weeks: in 1988 the period for loss of benefit will be increased to six months. The supplementary benefit paid to strikers' families has been cut, and a deduction is now made on the assumption that a union is paying strike pay, whether or not such a payment is actually made. In addition, those on strike do not receive any income-tax rebate due until a return to work or the end of the financial year, whichever is the sooner. The unemployed are now treated similarly by the Inland Revenue, with tax rebates being paid on re-employment or at the end of the financial year. In this respect the UK now treats the unemployed and strikers more harshly than it treats criminals sent to prison!

(4) Action on trade unions: while Minford's proposals to withdraw all immunities from the unions and to subject them to the common law have yet to be enacted, legislation in 1980, 1982 and 1984 has had an effect. Secondary picketing is now illegal, the funds of unions can be confiscated for certain actions, and secret ballots are compulsory before strike action. The powers of the trade unions have been dramatically reduced and, again, further changes are on the way. And if one links these changes with the effects of high unemployment on union membership in the UK and on union finances, it is clear that organised labour just does not enjoy the power and influence in the 1980s than it had in the 1970s.

(5) A myriad of special training schemes have been introduced for the unemployed in an attempt, it is said, to improve the quality of labour (see above). However, the quality of the schemes themselves is such that one really cannot treat this rather noble objective at face value. Training initiatives to date are largely cosmetic, aimed at reducing the unemployment count (see 7 below). As we saw in Chapter 2, none of the 700,000-plus unemployed people taking part in a special scheme at any time are counted among the registered unemployed. These training and retraining schemes reduce the unemployment total and give the unemployed something (anything?) to do.

(6) At 27 million the labour force in the UK has been growing (employed and unemployed). Action has been taken to reduce the supply of labour and the participation by some groups on the labour market. Special schemes by governments or individual employers that encourage earlier retirement can have this effect. Prolonging one's studies in school or college can reduce labour supply too. Cutbacks in child-care facilities and changes in employee taxation (such as the abolition of the reduced married woman's national insurance contribution or maintaining a high effective marginal rate of tax on low-paid or part-time work) will disproportionately affect female participation

in the labour force. Link this with the tough questioning of unemployed women with children about the instant availability of child-care and their own ready availability for work, then it is easy to see just how some groups might be dissuaded from actively pursuing a claim to participate in the labour force. This is independent of the exclusion of some groups (including women and the older claimant) from the registered unemployment total.

(7) Action has been taken on 'fine-tuning' the unemployment total. As noted above, those on special schemes are excluded from the count. The nineteen changes that have been made since 1979 to just how we count the unemployed have allegedly been made in the interests of statistical accuracy. We now only include benefit claimants, excluding those unemployed in any normal sense of the word and looking for a job, but ineligible for benefit. Men aged 60 and over on supplementary benefit are excluded. The details were discussed in Chapter 2.

It can be argued that these actions and proposed actions do represent a carefully considered strategy for the labour market. Having identified failings on the supply-side of the labour market as being mainly instrumental in causing the current high levels of unemployment, it has been necessary, the government would argue, to take remedial action at a pace that can be understood and absorbed. So, we have had much activity over the past eight years in order to reduce the reservation (minimum acceptable) wage of the unemployed, to reduce the value of benefits, to tighten up eligibility for benefit, to curb the influence of the trade unions, to strengthen labour discipline and give more powers to employers, to try and improve the quality of labour (particularly the reserve army of labour represented by the unemployed) and to cut labour supply. In addition, income tax cuts have attempted to increase the incentive to resume work or to stay in a job. The improved 'accuracy' of the unemployment count makes the unemployment mountain to be climbed somewhat less high! It is a coherent set of policies for the labour market and for unemployment.

But it will not work because the analysis of the main causes of unemployment is fundamentally flawed. Supply-side influences such as the benefit system, employment protection, trade union power, labour quality and quantity and so on are of course present. This is recognised by most of the neo-Keynesian economists and more generally by the government's critics. However, without action on the demand side of the economy, the changes outlined above are merely tinkering with the crisis of unemployment, while at the same time creating hardship and heartbreak for those afflicted.

CONCLUSIONS

This chapter has presented a number of differing explanations for the rise in unemployment to over 3 million in the 1980s, Some space has been devoted to the 'new' Keynesian explanation of cause, which identifies a chronic shortage of demand in the UK economy as being largely responsible for the crisis of unemployment that continues to confront us. Four-fifths of the increase in unemployment can be accounted for by demand factors. Government intervention on public expenditure and taxation, among other policy initiatives, can reduce this unemployment total to just 1 million. These neo-Keynesian policies to get Britain back to work are presented and discussed in Chapters 8 and 9, where a comprehensive programme of jobs for the 1990s is considered.

Rather more space in this chapter has been devoted to different ways of explaining why unemployment has risen. In brief, the problem is perceived more readily in terms of welfare benefits, wages and unions. The conclusions and proposals for cure by one leading economist are considered. The similarities between this supply-sider neo-classical view and the Thatcher government's analysis of the problem and the remedial action taken have to be emphasised. It has to be stated bluntly that they are wrong. Their explanation of why unemployment has risen so far so fast and stayed there is wrong. And while it is more than possible that the actions taken against benefit claimants, the low paid and the unions have more to do with a political rather than an economic objective, they cannot and will not reduce unemployment substantially.

We should ask ourselves this. If the government's long-standing assessment of the causes of the UK's high unemployment were correct, and if the actions taken to improve our jobs market can be justified on these terms, just why is it that after eight years, in 1987, registered unemployment stubbornly remains at the 3 million mark? All the actions reported above, on wages, on benefits, on labour discipline, on trade unions, on training and on labour supply have taken place. The unemployment figures themselves have also been carefully massaged. If the identification of the causes of high unemployment is correct, and the supply-side corrections made are the right ones, just why is unemployment remaining so high. It really should have been plummeting by now.

The reason why unemployment stays high is a simple one, but no less dispiriting for those who are unemployed. A coherent policy the government may have. But it is the wrong policy. Nothing short of urgent attention to the demand side of the economy can make substantial inroads into the unemployment problem.

The 1987 Conservative Party manifesto proclaimed that 'the fight against unemployment is being won'. It isn't. And what is promised for the future is more of the same.

4. Who Are the Unemployed?

They live in Petersfield, Preston and Perth. They are miners, brick-layers, personnel officers, sales assistants or teachers. They are 17, 32 or 50 years old. They are single, separated, or married, with or without children. They are black or white, male or female. There are 4 million of them: they were all unemployed in 1987. Half a million of them were unemployed in 1984. Most of all, the unemployed are people, are individuals, like you and me. They are not an anonymous seven-digit number that competes with other news items once a month on television, on the radio and in newspapers.

Of the 2.9 million registered unemployed claimants in June 1987, 70 per cent were men, 30 per cent women. This ratio of men to women has held pretty constantly throughout the 1980s. Of course, unemployed non-claimant women represent a far higher proportion of those looking for work, but they are currently not included in the official monthly count. This is mainly because if they have paid the reduced, married-woman's national insurance contribution they will be ineligible for benefit in their own right, are less likely to have sufficient contributions in the right time period, or have been employed part-time. For potential women claimants with young children, the tests of availability for work, particularly when it comes to instantly available and acceptable (to social security officials) child-care arrangements, have recently been tightened up.

For unemployed school-leavers (just 70,000 of the 2.9 million June 1987) the ratio between young men and women is more nearly equal, on average operating at about four young male school-leavers for every three young women. Given that school-leavers at present are unable to claim benefit until the September after leaving school, it is September that is the peak month for the unemployed school-leaver total each year. In September 1986 there were 80,000 young men and 60,000 young women unemployed who had left school that year.

Certainly, in the 1980s, young people entering the labour market have suffered disproportionately. Before embarking on a spate of redundancies or plant closures, employers will frequently cut back on recruitment or freeze recruitment altogether. This has especially serious consequences for those looking for their first jobs. Rather perversely, government attempts to tackle youth unemployment through the introduction and expansion of the Youth Training Scheme has had the effect of reducing the number of 'real' jobs and non-YTS traineeships on offer, as companies have substituted YTS trainees for school-leaver recruitment of trainees. The Manpower Services Commission estimates that 50,000 jobs have been lost in this way. Other estimates, and studies of company behaviour, put this figure much higher.

In the succeeding months, as school-leavers join the YTS, return to school or college or get jobs, the figures fall. The year 1987 was the final one in which any young school-leavers will be included in the unemployment count at all, since it is proposed that benefit be refused those not accepting a YTS place. It was only a matter of time before compulsion became the order of the day: once there were sufficient YTS places for all 16- and 17-year-olds, and in the right locations, the Conservative acceptance of a 'workfare' philosophy (i.e. you 'work' for your welfare payments) meant that participation in YTS would be mandatory. A similar strategy towards an expansion of places on other special schemes for the unemployed (e.g. Job Training Scheme or the Community Programme) linked with compulsory attendance could reduce the official unemployment count to zero!

Table 4.1 shows the ages of the registered unemployed. On average, unemployed women tend to be younger than their male counterparts. Two-thirds of unemployed women are under the age of 35, with 40 per cent under the age of 25. One-half of unemployed men are under the age of 35, one-half older than this.

Even according to the official figures, 1.3 million people have been unemployed for over a year, 990,000 men and over 300,000 women. While people do come in and out of unemployment each month, for the vast majority of the unemployed they do, regrettably, have a reasonably substantial experience of being unemployed with all that this means (see Chapter 5). Over two in

ages of the unemployed: percentage of the total
ed population in each age band, UK, April 1987

Age	Men %	Women %	All %
Under 18	3	6	4
18–19	7	12	9
20–24	19	23	20
25–34	25	25	25
35–44	17	13	16
45–54	15	13	14
55–59	10	8	10
60 and over	3	1	2
Total per cent	100	100	100
Total number	2,158,200	948,900	3,107,100

five of the total unemployed have now been so for over a year. An
additional one in five have been jobless for between six months
and a year. (We used to consider six months and over as being
long-term unemployment.) A further 15 per cent have been
unemployed for between 13 and 26 weeks. So, for three-quarters of
the unemployed, they have been out of work for three months or
longer. Some politicians have laid great emphasis on the way
unemployment is often a short-term phenomenon, emphasising
the flows of unemployment on and off the register rather than the
large stock of unemployed and wasted talent. In fact, just 9 per
cent of the unemployed have been jobless for less than four weeks.
And so very often these weeks do stretch out into months, and in
some cases, years. Nearly 300,000 young men and women aged
under 25 have been unemployed for more than a year.

We saw in Chapter 2 how the unemployed are not evenly
distributed around the country. Where you live and what you do
for a living make a considerable difference to your likelihood of
becoming unemployed and your prospects for re-employment
once out of work. Within a UK official unemployment figure now
at 10.5 per cent of the *working population*, the broad-brush regional
figure for the south-east is 7.4 per cent, albeit going much higher
(and much lower) than this in places. The average for the north-
west of England is 13.3 per cent, for the north of England 14.6 per
cent and for Northern Ireland 18.3 per cent (June 1987 figures).
Strabane in Northern Ireland has the unhappy experience of
having an unemployment rate of over one-third. The Department

of Employment's *Employment Gazette* publishes local unemployment figures by region, county, local authority district and by parliamentary constituency. Statistics are also available on the likelihood of becoming unemployed by age, region and gender. In addition, calculations are made on the likelihood of an unemployed person ceasing to be unemployed. So, from January to April 1987, the average chance of becoming unemployed was 4 per cent, or one in 25. But if you were aged 25 to 29 years your chances were one in 20. In the north of England or Scotland there would be 5.5 per cent likelihood of an individual being becoming unemployed during this period. The likelihood of becoming unemployed in 1986 and 1987 was, unsurprisingly, lowest in the south-east and East Anglia.

As we saw in Chapter 2, the regional mix of occupations and industries has meant that those localities and regions more than averagely dependent on manufacturing and primary industries have been experiencing the most adverse unemployment problem. The occupational effects of this have been just as pervasive as the industrial and regional effects. When it has come to 'correcting overmanning' or 'producing leaner and fitter employing organisations', both euphemisms for sacking people, those groups of employees most likely to lose their jobs have been those in skilled, semi-skilled or unskilled manual or 'blue collar' jobs. Managers

Table 4.2: Percentage of men aged 18–64 experiencing unemployment in previous 12 months in 1984

Occupational group	No spells of unemployment	One spell of unemployment	Two or more spells of unemployment	Total %
Professional, employers and managers	94	6	0	100
Intermediate, junior, non-manual	88	11	1	100
All non-manual	92	8	1	100
Skilled manual	83	15	2	100
Semi-skilled and unskilled manual	71	24	4	100
All manual	79	18	3	100
All men	84	14	2	100

Source: *General Household Survey*, 1984.

and professionals, many of whom have actually been making the decisions on just who to sack, when, and at what particular factories and plants, have been secure in employment by comparison.

Table 4.2, from the 1984 *General Household Survey*, shows that only 6 per cent of male managers and professionals experienced a spell of unemployment over the 12 months 1983–4. Among skilled manual workers 17 per cent had experienced one or more spells of unemployment, and 28 per cent of semi- and unskilled workers had been unemployed at least once. So, for managers and the like, there was a one in 16 chance that they would experience being without a job. At the other extreme, for the semi- and unskilled male worker, the risk was one in 4. There has been, and is, a sharp contrast between the different occupational groups in their familiarity with unemployment. As an accountant, or a personnel manager or a university lecturer, you are so much less likely to have any experience of unemployment at all than if you are a building labourer or a machine minder in metal fabrication. As a member of the professional and managerial group, should you be unfortunate enough to be without work, then on average, the length of time you will stay unemployed will also be much less than those with manual skills or with no special vocational skills at all. And, as we have seen, where you live also makes a substantial difference.

There are differences in unemployment rates and chances between different ethnic groups. According to the 1985 *Labour Force Survey* under 11 per cent of economically active white males aged between 16 and 64 years were out of work at the time of the survey. (Economically active includes full-time and part-time employees, the self-employed, those on special schemes and those out of employment but looking for work.) The unemployment figure for West Indian and Guyanese men was more than double that of white males at 23 per cent. The Indian, Pakistani and Bangladeshi figure was 22 per cent. The unemployment rates of these non-white female groups was much higher, as Figure 4.1 shows.

While part of these differences can be explained in terms of the qualifications, skills, industrial grouping and age-profile of the different ethnic groups, these factors just cannot explain all the differences. There remains racial discrimination in the UK labour market in the hiring and firing of employees, that seems exacerbated in times of high unemployment. Indeed, if close attention is just paid to employees and the unemployed (full-time and part-time employees but excluding the self-employed and those on government schemes) then the unemployment rate amongst West Indian men rises to over 25 per cent, and for the Indian and Pakistani group to 27 per cent. On this indicator unemployment among white men rises to 12 per cent. Figure 4.2 shows those out

Figure 4.1: Employment and unemployment among the economically active, by ethnic origin, in 1985. Men aged 16–64, women aged 16–59

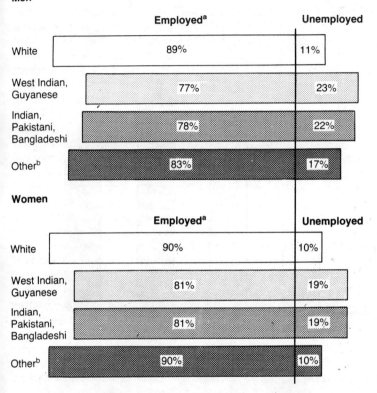

Men

	Employed[a]	Unemployed
White	89%	11%
West Indian, Guyanese	77%	23%
Indian, Pakistani, Bangladeshi	78%	22%
Other[b]	83%	17%

Women

	Employed[a]	Unemployed
White	90%	10%
West Indian, Guyanese	81%	19%
Indian, Pakistani, Bangladeshi	81%	19%
Other[b]	90%	10%

Note: a. Includes self-employed, part-time employees and special schemes.
b. Other includes African, Arab, Chinese, mixed.
Source: *Labour Force Survey*, 1985.

of employment as a percentage of the labour force (employees and the unemployed added together). According to the government's *General Household Survey*, too, white males have a lower propensity to experience unemployment than have non-white groups. In the year to the time of the survey in 1984, 16 per cent of white men had one or more spells of unemployment. The figure for 'coloured' men was 26 per cent. (Note: 'coloured' is in quotes here because the classification is based on the interviewers' assessments of skin colour! This is not the same as ethnic origin.)

Figure 4.2: Unemployment among men aged 16–64 in different ethnic groups in 1985

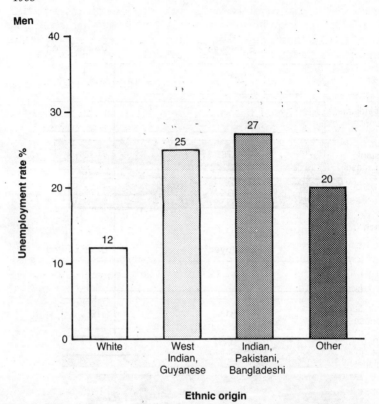

Men

In the ethnic minority communities, unemployment is especially severe among young people. The 1985 *Labour Force Survey* found that over a third of all ethnic-minority young people were out of work (aged 16–24). This compares with 16 per cent of the white population of the same age. West Indian young people had an unemployment rate approaching 40 per cent; Pakistani and Bangladeshi ethnic groups under 25 years of age experienced a 35 per cent unemployment rate. In 1987 there have been no marked improvements in their situation. But, of course, we have it on the very best authority that high youth unemployment is in no way related to inner city riots! These are the very same authorities who also refuse to accept the links between unemployment and poor physical and mental health (see Chapter 5).

Unemployment is a regional problem. It is an industrial and occupational problem. It is related to age and gender issues. But unemployment is also concerned with race discrimination.

CONCLUSIONS

It can be seen that we do know rather a lot about the unemployed. There is information on their previous jobs (if they had one), their skills, where they live, their gender and some data on ethnic origin, the latter from social surveys. This information is important.

Policy measures designed to reduce unemployment must have in their sights those who are currently jobless, and those who are at the greatest risk of becoming unemployed in the future. It is useless to bid for a great expansion of, say, professional jobs in the public services if there are no suitably qualified and experienced people available to fill them. An expansion of further and higher education to fill such vacancies can only be justified (in terms of reducing unemployment) if simultaneously there is a rapid increase in the demand for complementary services than can offer work to the unemployed. A growth in the output from medical schools, for example, can only be deemed acceptable if National Health Service manpower planning and budgets permit the employment of more doctors *and*, most importantly for unemployment alleviation, this leads to a substantial increase in the number of unskilled and semi-skilled jobs available in ancillary health care. There are similar examples in the other public services.

As far as regional differences in unemployment are concerned, regional aid that just gives grant assistance for capital equipment or subsidies on buildings has to be misplaced if full account is not taken of the number of new jobs created. Any unemployment-alleviation measures, such as public-expenditure increases, job subsidies and the rest, have to be targeted. Crawley, in West Sussex, currently has an unemployment rate of 3.7 per cent. What sense is it to embark on blanket job-creation measures that will affect Crawley to a similar extent as Merseyside? None at all.

In short, then, the information that exists on who are the unemployed can act as a guide in the formulation of policies and programmes to reduce unemployment. The long-term unemployed everywhere are a special target group; young people everywhere are another one. Priority programmes have to be mounted for the semi-skilled and unskilled manual worker, for the ethnic minorities and in those localities (including the inner cities) where unemployment is especially high. The blanket application of policies, including income tax cuts for those in work, are wasteful and inefficient. They do not have as their target those experiencing the corrosive effects of unemployment in 1988.

5.

The Personal Experience of Unemployment

Unemployment has severe consequences for the person who becomes unemployed. In debates about the global statistics of unemployment—who should be counted as being unemployed, the accuracy of the unemployment count and changes in definitions—it is all too easy to lose sight of the fact that for any unemployed individual unemployment is 100 per cent. The media in its different guises gives headline attention to the monthly unemployment totals, commonly ignoring the personal histories of poverty, deprivation, ill-health, marital breakdown, homelessness and sapped motivation so often associated with unemployment, particularly long-term unemployment.

Comparisons are sometimes made between the personal experience of unemployment in the 1930s and the experience of the jobless in the 1980s. Fifty years on, certainly the crude numbers of people unemployed are similar. But as a proportion of the labour force, unemployment is lower now. The composition of the labour force and the unemployed is very different, however, with registered unemployment among women, young people and the ethnic minorities much less pronounced in the 1930s. The similarities are concerned with those parts of the UK most adversely affected by unemployment, the higher propensity of the unskilled and semi-skilled worker to lose his or her job, and the ways in which the older-established, more traditional industries have borne the brunt of the unemployment increase. Shipbuilding, steel, the extractive industries, construction and manufacturing have been especially hard hit since the late 1970s.

The post-1945 period has seen a further breakdown of supportive networks for the unemployed. The geographical dispersal of families, in particular, sometimes aided by redeployment policies, has led to the increasing isolation of the unemployed. As George Orwell has commented: 'Unemployment is a disaster that happens to you as an individual and for which you are to blame'.

This individualisation of unemployment is aided and abetted by both politicians and the media. Politicians point out that the unemployed are to blame for their own predicament, by not being fully mobile, by not taking one of the low-paid or part-time jobs on offer, by not acquiring the skills that would give them a greater chance of work, by being less productive in the past than their foreign counterparts, and by demanding pay rises. If you are unemployed it is your own fault, the script runs. The governments of the 1980s can only create the conditions in which enterprise can flourish and you have to take your chances. The media approach is different. The popular image of the unemployed is of feckless wastrels, dole scroungers, a sea of voluntarily unemployed people living well off the backs of the hard-working tax-payer, and probably supplementing their overgenerous unemployment benefit with illicit, undeclared work in the hidden economy. Faced with such a barrage of ignorant and unsubstantiated comment it is little wonder that the unemployed feel isolated.

The television, radio and written media also perform another function in influencing the lives of the unemployed. As well the portrayal of the unemployed as workshy, the media, and television in particular, present powerful images of consumerism. They continually remind the unemployed that they are failing to provide themselves and their children with the fashionable consumer goods or latest convenience foods available. One in nine children live in families where the head of the household is unemployed. Commercial television daily bombards these families and their more fortunate friends with advertisements for all the latest and most desirable toys and activities for children. Just how do you respond at the time of your child's birthday or at the approach of Christmas to such consumerism pressures?

The rest of this chapter is concerned with the ways in which the experience of unemployment affects income levels and the health and well-being of individuals and families. The human costs of unemployment have been summarised by Charter for Jobs, an organisation that seeks a return to high employment levels. In six bleak statements of fact, Charter for Jobs has summarised the conclusions of a plethora of social research in this area:

- Unemployment is a corrosive experience for most people.
- The picture of the unemployed as wealthy 'dole scroungers' could not be further from the truth. The normal consequences of not being able to get a job is increased poverty.
- Unemployment does not just mean loss of income. Work provides an accepted way of satisfying many human needs.
- Denial of access to work and income can lead to a deterioration in both physical and mental health, and in extreme cases death.
- Loss of job places many strains on the families of the unemployed. Partners and children suffer mentally and physically. Families can break up.
- Unemployment costs the country dearly through lost output and lost taxes. But it is the individual who bears the worst scars.

Source: Charter for Jobs (1986) *Economic Report*, volume 2, number 1.

UNEMPLOYMENT AND POVERTY

Unemployment, and the reliance of the unemployed on benefit, leads to a massive drop in the standard of living of those losing their jobs. Temporary relief may be available for those who receive some redundancy pay from their employers, but for those not eligible and solely and immediately rely on unemployment and supplementary benefit, the onset of unemployment means the onset of a low income. The longer the duration of unemployment the worse the situation becomes. Evidence from the Department of Health and Social Security (DHSS) showed that for half of the men becoming unemployed their benefit replaced less than one-half of their previous take-home pay. And in spite of the popular images of a financially comfortable life on the dole, just one in 20 was actually better off from being unemployed than in his previous job.

Over the years a number of social-research studies have been carried out to determine the extent to which individuals becoming unemployed are worse (or better) off out of work than they were in a job. This kind of work has had an important policy objective. As long ago as 1941 Burns wrote that one of the most important policy issues to settle was the balance that had to be drawn between providing sufficient income for the unemployed to guarantee an adequate standard of living, while at the same time maintaining the wage incentive; that is, ensuring that there was a positive financial incentive for the unemployed to return to work as quickly as possible. It is argued later on that most of the arguments in favour of protecting the wage incentive are in fact illusory ones.

Economists and social-policy analysts in this examination of incomes in and out of work often engage in the calculation of what are called replacement ratios. These replacement ratios show what proportion of previous income is 'replaced' by benefits when people become unemployed. There are two main reasons why these comparisons of wages and salaries and unemployment benefits are important. First, we do need to subject income levels during spells of unemployment to close scrutiny to see whether or not benefit levels are sufficient to meet the needs of unemployed people and the extent to which they can come close to maintaining their standards of living. The second reason for comparing incomes in this way is to examine the extent to which benefit levels for the unemployed *might* create a disincentive to work.

Over the past ten years much greater attention has been paid to this second reason for calculating replacement ratios than to the first. At the policy and political levels it seems as if the relief of poverty amongst the unemployed rates very poorly as an objective in comparison with maintaining financial pressure on the unemployed to get back to work—even if there is very little work to get back to.

The issue of maintaining incentives can be considered in two ways. It is felt necessary to monitor income and benefit levels in order to ensure that benefits are not pitched at so generous a level that the unemployed do not experience a marked disincentive to return to work once they are jobless. In addition, the differentials between employment and unemployment have to be maintained, it is argued, so that there is no incentive for those with work to voluntarily quit their jobs to take advantage of benefit levels that might be higher than their wages or salaries. In fact, up until the mid-1970s it was not possible for unemployed people to receive more in benefit than they had received in work, through the wage-stop regulation. The operation of this benefit-capping arrangement, together with earnings-related unemployment benefit had the effect of ensuring that those in poverty whilst at work remained in poverty when out of work. The abolition of the rule that restricted benefit to a maximum of previous earnings seems to have had little effect. Whether it was in the 1960s, 1970s or 1980s, only a small minority of people would ever be better off financially out of work than in it.

Before turning to the evidence on unemployment and income levels, it is worth briefly discussing the different kinds of assessment that can be carried out in looking at incomes in and out of work. The reasons for such exercises have already been explained. There are two main types of replacement ratios that can be calculated. There are those of a hypothetical nature that will make assumptions about non-existent households but with typical characteristics of family size, housing costs, earnings levels and so on, and will go on to compute the extent to which benefits can take the place of these hypothetical earnings. Of much more value are the empirical studies of actual unemployed people that will look at their financial position in and out of work. These empirical studies can take the form of either just looking at the actual benefits paid and comparing this with earnings while at work, or considering the total household income when in work with total income when out of work, including benefit. This does make a difference.

One of the most recent and most comprehensive studies of earnings and benefits was carried out by the DHSS in 1978, albeit published some years later. For 94 per cent of the unemployed men included in the survey, take-home pay while in work exceeded unemployment benefits, and for half of these men the gap was greater than £20 a week. For almost half of the unemployed, their standard of living had more than halved on becoming unemployed, such is the nature of the welfare-payments system for the unemployed.

In common with all the studies of this kind carried out from the late 1930s to the present time, the Department of Health and Social Security did find a small proportion of unemployed men rather better off on the dole—6 per cent. So, for some one in 20 of those unemployed men in the very late 1970s, benefits exceeded previous net earnings. This figure is in the same order as other findings published in the earlier 1970s and the 1980s. So, for example, a study published in the Department of Employment *Gazette* in 1974 found 7 per cent better off out of work. In 1983 a study on long-term unemployment published by the Policy Studies Institute also found 7 per cent with a higher income out of work. A 1982 study quoted by Jahoda estimated that just 2 per cent had higher incomes from unemployment benefits than from their previous jobs. The average benefit level for those unemployed for short periods replaced 58 per cent of their previous earnings. For the long-term unemployed average benefit amounted to 43 per cent of previous income.

In 1987 the DHSS again carried out detailed interviews with the unemployed, in a part replica of the 1978 study. On this occasion the assessment of earnings and benefits (and much else besides) includes unemployed women and men, and it will be interesting to see what conclusions are reached. The changes that have taken place to the welfare rights of the unemployed since 1979, which include the taxation of unemployment benefits, together with the much faster rate of growth of earnings in comparison with benefits in the 1980s, lead to an expectation that only a tiny proportion of the unemployed, if any, will now be financially better-off out of work. However, if any claimants prove to have their previous earnings replaced by benefits at a level at or over 100 per cent, then the government may well look even more sympathetically at proposals that would, once again, cap benefit entitlement to some

Table 5.1: The shortfall between net weekly earnings and the
unemployment benefits of unemployed men

		Per cent
Weekly earnings higher than benefits	Total	94
£		
by more than 50		12
40–50		7
30–40		11
20–30		19
10–20		27
5–10		12
under 5		6
Weekly benefits higher than earnings	Total	6
£		
by up to 5		3
5–10		2
over 10		1

Source: Department of Health and Social Security, *For Richer, For Poorer*,
1984.

fixed proportion of previous earnings. The most prominent
proposal along these lines comes from Patrick Minford at Liverpool
University, whose other policy ideas for the unemployed have
been influential in the 1980s. A main corner-stone of the Minford
package of reforms is to limit unemployment benefits to 70 per cent
of previous earnings. Further evidence, such as that from the 1987
DHSS survey, which may continue to show a proportion of the
unemployed better-off out of work, is likely to lead to the adoption
of a wage stop of this kind. This would push the unemployed
further into poverty, since its impact would be felt by those in the
lowest-paid and least secure jobs in the economy.

It is already the case that the income-drop experienced by the
unemployed can be very large indeed. Table 5.1 reproduces
evidence from the DHSS study *For Richer, For Poorer*. More than
one in ten unemployed men experience a drop in their incomes of
more than £50 a week on becoming unemployed. For one-third the
drop was £30 or more. In contrast, just 1 per cent gained £10 a
week or more from becoming unemployed.

These figures refer only to the take-home pay and benefits of the
men becoming unemployed. Reference was made earlier to the
way household income is sometimes included in the calculation of
income-replacement ratios. When the rather broader family
income is assessed the picture changes somewhat, with benefits

Table 5.2: Income replacement ratios of unemployed men[a], per cent

Percentage of working income replaced	Columns	
	A	B
No benefit received out of work	3	1
Under 25	10	7
25–49	33	27
50–79	39	40
80–99	10	16
100 or more	6	9

Note: a. Percentage of previous net earnings (column A) or household income (column B) replaced by benefits and other income when out of work for three months or more.

and income from other sources (including spouse's income, if any) replacing rather more of previous income from all sources. In Table 5.2, column A shows the relationship between benefits and net earnings (as in Table 5.1), and column B includes other household income.

The easiest way to interpret Table 5.2 is by means of an example. The 33 in column A means that for 33 per cent of unemployed men, unemployment benefits made up between 25 and 49 per cent of their previous earnings. The 6 per cent at the foot of column A represents those men who received 100 per cent or more of their previous earnings as benefit. These are the same 6 per cent in Table 5.1 whose benefits were higher than earnings. Column B includes income other than earnings and benefits for both in work and out of work.

The inclusion of other household income shows 9 per cent of benefit recipients receiving the same or more than they had previously received at work. However, over the medium term we do know there is a high tendency for an employed spouse to give up work once the household head has been unemployed for a year or more. Only 30 per cent of unemployed male heads of household have working spouses. This compares with nearly 60 per cent of employed male household heads. The longer the duration of the husband's unemployment the lower the tendency of a wife in work to continue in paid employment. The benefit system, along with other factors, positively discourages the continuation of a one-in/one-out arrangement of family employment.

We know then, that the vast majority of unemployed people experience a large drop in their incomes on becoming unemployed.

In the past, a small minority have become better off financially, and this has partly been because when in work they have failed to claim benefit due to them as low-paid employees such as Family Income Supplement, and partly because while the labour-market reward system does not recognise different family responsibilities and financial needs among employees, the welfare-payments system does take cognisance of such differences.

However, whatever the reasons, we do have to recognise that some individuals do experience rather less financial hardship on losing their jobs than they experienced in work. But to move from this recognition to a bald conclusion of fact that these individuals will be experiencing a marked disincentive effect to return to employment is to make heroic and doubtful assertions about the motivation for work. One cannot slip easily from the evidence of 100 per cent-plus income-replacement ratios for some, to the conclusion that this group will choose to stay voluntarily unemployed just because their incomes are somewhat higher when unemployed. To do so fundamentally misunderstands the role of work and the status of employment in a country such as the UK.

The evidence is overwhelming that unemployment causes real financial hardship to those affected. All research in this area points to the same conclusions. And yet the main focus of policy research, particularly from government departments is on the alleged disincentive effects of the welfare-benefits system. Much less attention is given to the way existing levels of benefit patently fail to provide for a standard of living that most of those fortunate enough to be in employment would regard as adequate. The position for those with children is especially severe: some 1.3 million children under the age of 16 now live in families where the head of the household is unemployed. Work by Richard Berthoud of the Policy Studies Institute demonstrates clearly how benefit levels are just too low to provide for basic human needs. Of couples with children relying on supplementary benefit, one-half ran out of money most weeks. Six families in ten did not possess a complete standard set of clothing. Fifty-two per cent were in debt. A quarter of those unemployed for under a year require the assistance of supplementary benefit to top up any unemployment benefit received. The 1.3 million people unemployed for over a year are all dependent on supplementary benefit.

This section on unemployment and poverty has so far been rather relying on averages and broad-brush statistics. This provides us with evidence necessary to debunk notions of over-generous unemployment benefits and the media image of the happy and relaxed dole scroungers. But underneath these statistics lie millions of often harrowing personal experiences of the impact of unemployment. These individual histories are not intended to be representative (although there is little doubt that they are experiences shared by many), but they do give us a good insight into life on the dole in the 1980s.

DAVID'S HISTORY

David was made redundant in 1983. An operator in a metal-fabrication factory in the West Midlands, he was not too surprised when the company went into receivership. Orders had been lost to cheaper foreign imports and there was a general awareness among the workforce that business was pretty bad. Earlier rounds of voluntary and then compulsory redundancies had made David feel more optimistic about the future. After all, the workforce had been halved, but he was still there. He thought he was one of the lucky ones. It soon became apparent, however, that those remaining when the receiver was called in were in fact the unlucky ones. Instead of receiving redundancy that would have amounted to three times the statutory minimum, David's claim for redundancy compensation became just one line in the very long list of company creditors. He ended up by receiving the state minimum.

> When the company went bust I wasn't too worried. After all I had seen my mates leave the year before with pretty good redundancy money. I thought I would do alright, too, after being there 18 years. I also thought I could get another job OK too.
> It was a bit of a blow when I found the redundancy money was only enough to pay off the HP on the car and a few bits and pieces.

David is married, aged 38 and with two children at primary school. In 1987 he is still unemployed. He still remembers the first experience of claiming benefit.

> I'd never been on the dole before. Been in the same job since leaving school. The first time I went to get my dole was so depressing. I felt so guilty, going in there and getting money for doing nothing. They made you feel guilty too. All those questions.

Before becoming unemployed himself David had not had much time for the unemployed. His own view reflected that of his daily newspaper.

> Bloody scroungers I thought. They don't want a job, living it up on the dole. Even my mates from [company name] who'd left, I

really thought that if they tried to find a job they could get one OK. It was only when I tried, and I bloody well tried hard, it was only then that I found out what it was really like. Nothing doing.

David says he tried extremely hard to find work during the first year or so out of work. As time went on, still without success, his motivation to find work lessened considerably.

At first I went for everything. Doing anything. I'd travel, do nights, shifts, whatever. There wasn't that much going anyway and everybody was after the same jobs. After a bit you sort of give up. I still go down the Jobcentre and there's a few more cards now, but not much for me.

Even when something apparently suitable does get reported to the Jobcentre, the fact that David has been unemployed for four years certainly counts against him. In the competition for job vacancies employers seemingly prefer the new entrants to the labour market (e.g. school-leavers, YTS trainees etc), or the short-term unemployed.

It's as if there's something wrong with you, as if you've got AIDS or something. Four years on the dole and a lot of them [employers] write you off as soon as you walk in door. I've done the Community Programme but that was a waste of time. I'm supposed to be going on some kind of training scheme soon. That might help.

Training schemes and possible employment are for the future. David and his family's experience of unemployment so far indicate just how excluded you can be from the rest of society: poor and with lots of time on your hands to brood.

I earnt good money at [company name]. When I first got my dole money I thought they'd made a mistake. I went and told them 'We can't live on this'. But it wasn't any mistake. With a bit of redundancy money and a bit of savings I guess we did alright at the beginning. But then the money went and stuff wore out. I sold the car. Now its just the dole and the wife does a bit of cleaning.

The kids get it worse. We go to the jumble and stuff to try and get presents for them birthdays and things. They never get nothing new. Their school clothes have been mended so many times . . . I'm sure they don't eat proper except at school. I know we don't. Katie, that's our eldest, she's eleven, she'd really like to buy records and clothes like her friends now. But there's no money. I don't need anybody telling me to get a job. Just seeing our kids is enough to make me try hard for everything.

JOHN'S HISTORY

John left school in 1986 and joined the Youth Training Scheme. He did apply for, and was interviewed for several jobs, but was unsuccessful. He is hoping that participation on YTS will help him get permanent employment, perhaps with his current 'employer'. He lives at home with his parents.

> Most of my friends got jobs. I tried hard but didn't get many qualifications—a couple of CSEs. Most of the jobs seem to want more than that.
> YTS is OK. It's quite interesting. The worst thing is the money. My friends are passing their driving tests, getting cars, going out of an evening, taking girls out. I can't afford any of that. I give me mum £5 a week and I've got to buy clothes and things. I try and get out one night a week with my friends, but it's difficult to keep up. If we go out, to a pub or something, buying rounds, one round wipes me out for the week. I just can't keep up.

John is extremely worried in case he does not manage to secure a 'proper job' during or at the end of his YTS placement. Part of this concern is associated with the continued low level of income he would have to endure without full-time employment. His lifestyle would continue to be at odds with that of his friends. John keenly feels his exclusion from the activities of his peers now at work. They are making plans that, at present, he cannot share.

> I want to go out more, to have girlfriends. I'm young yet, but obviously some time I will want to get married, buy a house, have kids, and that. If I don't get a job then I'm where I am now. My friends will have all that and I'll just be, well, living at home I guess. As long as they put up with me!

JOANNE'S HISTORY

Joanne has three children and is divorced. She is totally dependent on supplementary benefit for her income. She holds her husband's unemployment in 1980 as being responsible for the breakdown of her marriage. He now lives in a hostel for homeless men.

Everything was all right. We had three lovely kids, nice house, car. Geoff had a good job, production supervisor. Then he got the sack for stealing from the factory. He didn't go to court, they didn't press charges, but obviously he lost the job.

That's when the trouble started. He couldn't get another job, losing his other one like that. We went from over £200 a week down to about £80. We just couldn't manage. We had such rows about money.

Geoff gave up applying for jobs pretty quick. With stealing like that he couldn't get another job and really didn't see the point of trying. He'd just sit around the house all day, moping. He started getting nasty with the kids and with me, shouting if they made a noise or asked for sweets or toys. It was terrible.

I put up with all that for about a year then I left with the kids. I went back to my parents for a bit and then got possession of the house. It's better now without him but I still have trouble making ends meet . . .

The time I really dread is Christmas. The kids all want what their friends have, but I just can't afford it. They usually get one thing new—usually clothes—and then I fill the stocking with fruit and a few sweets and bits and pieces friends and relatives give me. You can see the disappointment on the kids' faces come Christmas Day but it's the best I can do. I just hope they'll understand when they're older.

UNEMPLOYMENT AND HEALTH

It is well documented that the unemployed have a much higher incidence of ill-health than those in work. From the Pilgrim Trust study in the 1930s to social research being carried out in the late 1980s this association between unemployment and the incidence of sickness is confirmed. The government's annual *General Household Survey* findings also reinforce this conclusion. The figures for those reporting a long-standing illness are 40 per cent higher for the unemployed than for the employed, and the figure for those with a 'limiting' long-standing illness is some 80 per cent higher. One of the most important reports on health and ill-health, the Health Education Council's 1987 publication *The Health Divide* concluded that:

The unemployed and their families have considerably worse physical and mental health than those in work. Until recently direct evidence that unemployment caused this was not available. Now there is substantial evidence of unemployment causing a deterioration in mental health with improvements observed on re-occupation.

69

Certainly, until relatively recently, while the link between unemployment and ill-health was not disputed, there was no agreement on the extent to which unemployment *caused* ill-health and, for some commentators and academics, there were two other hypotheses that could have fitted the evidence of association between poor health and unemployment. First, it could be that poorer health is the lot of the unemployed because those not in good health are most likely to become unemployed and then have most difficulty in regaining employment. The second possible explanation for the link was that those becoming unemployed on average had lower earnings when in work and experienced poorer housing conditions. This position was perpetuated and even worsened with the onset of unemployment. Up until the 1980s it was extremely difficult for social research to distinguish between the different explanations of the *proven* link between ill-health and unemployment.

The evidence of cause and effect is now so overwhelming that there is no doubt that for a substantial minority the experience of unemployment causes a worsening of physical and mental health. Evidence of the widening health gap between the unemployed and those in work is contained in a survey of 22,000 people carried out by Heartbeat Wales. The long-term unemployed were found to have the greatest incidence of high blood pressure, obesity, smoking and alcohol-related problems. The unemployed drank more alcohol and smoked more, while taking less exercise than those in work. The long-term unemployed developed unhealthy lifestyles because of being unemployed. Low-income families, including the unemployed, ate more unhealthy foods than other groups, the Heartbeat Wales report concluded. The British Regional Heart Study of 7500 men in 24 towns found that heart disease was significantly higher among unemployed men that those with jobs, even when you excluded those out of work because of poor health.

The government's Office of Population Censuses and Surveys (OPCS) followed up men unemployed at the time of the 1971 Census for ten years. Their mortality rate was 21 per cent higher than what would normally be expected. This exercise took into account differences in death rates between different occupational groups. Unemployment does not only affect the mortality rates of the unemployed themselves, it would seem. The OPCS found that the wives of the unemployed men being followed up in this way also experienced a death rate 20 per cent higher than normal. Preliminary results from a similar OPCS exercise being carried out after the 1981 Census shows the same pattern. As the Health Education Council have pointed out these studies reveal 'excess mortality in the unemployed which cannot easily be explained away'.

The 1980 Black Report on inequalities in health pointed to a widening in health differences between different groups and different areas. The updated research by the Health Education Council, and published in March 1987, concluded that the health gap identified by Sir Douglas Black had widened further. The differences were particularly pronounced between deprived and affluent areas, and between those in and out of work. *The Health Divide* report concluded that all the major killer diseases affect the poorest occupational groups more than the better off. The unskilled are more than twice as likely to die before the age of 64 than professionals. The babies of unskilled fathers run twice the risk of stillbirth and death under one year old.

The medical profession, too, have weighed in with their own review of the research evidence on ill-health, poverty and unemployment. A British Medical Association (BMA) discussion paper, again published in 1987, concluded that unemployment, poor housing and low incomes were causing substantial amounts of ill-health in Britain. *Deprivation and Ill-Health* reported 'clear evidence' that unemployment was associated with higher mortality rates. It went on to confirm that unemployed people were more prone to self-destructive behaviour, including suicide and drug-taking. The paper concluded that some psychiatric illness was *directly caused* by unemployment.

This is important. Given the increased poverty and sharp drop in the standard of living experienced by the vast majority of unemployed people and their families, it is not surprising to find evidence of poorer physical health among the unemployed, especially those remaining out of work for a year or longer. This poorer health is compounded by the effects of unemployment on their mental health. The mental-health effects can be even more insidious. Regrettably, here too the evidence is overwhelming that unemployment causes a deterioration in mental health.

The BMA found that unemployed school leavers had worse mental health than former peers at school who had managed to find work. The Health Education Council report *The Health Divide* reports on an Edinburgh study that found unemployed people six times more likely than the average to try to kill themselves during the first six months of unemployment. They were ten times more likely to attempt suicide during their following six months of unemployment. After a year on the dole they were *nineteen* times more likely to attempt suicide.

The 1987 Annual meeting of the British Association for the Advancement of Science was the venue for the presentation of the latest information from Edinburgh on the link between mental health, attempted suicide and unemployment. Edinburgh University's Dr Stephen Platt, in a detailed analysis of parasuicide (attempted suicide), found that those unemployed for a year or

Figure 5.1: How unemployment can affect health

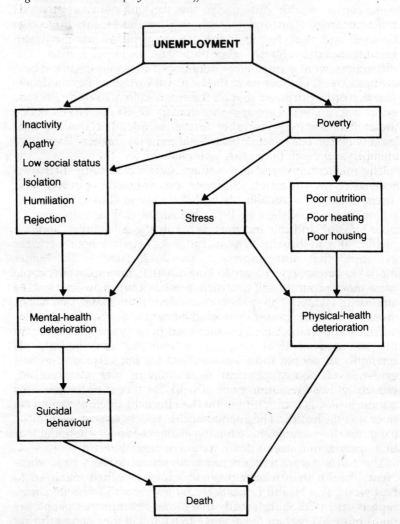

Source: Charter for Jobs.

more were twelve times more likely to deliberately injure themselves or attempt suicide than those with jobs. Even a short spell of unemployment can have an effect, with a three-fold increase in the rate of attempted suicide amongst those unemployed for less than four weeks. Unemployment leads to increased family tensions, arguments and sometimes violence. The situation is exacerbated by feelings of hopelessness, loss of self-esteem, depression and loss of confidence. Dr Platt argued that the high risk of attempted suicide among the unemployed might be ameliorated by devoting increased resources to assist the economic, social and psychological impact of prolonged unemployment.

Unemployment is implicated not only in attempting suicide but also in successful suicide as well. The Royal College of Psychiatrists have pointed to the way suicide among men has risen by 30 per cent in the last ten years, now accounting for 3000 deaths a year. About 1500 women a year also commit suicide. The Dean of the Royal College of Psychiatrists believes that higher levels of unemployment offers a part explanation for the increase in suicides: 'Unemployment has made a contribution to the increase in suicide rates among men. Men see their status more in terms of their job than do women'.

CONCLUSIONS

The evidence is overwhelming. Unemployment is responsible for a deterioration in physical and mental well-being. The longer the duration of unemployment the worse the situation becomes. The poverty of the unemployed and their physical-health state are inextricably linked. Any savings or redundancy pay are quickly eaten away with total dependence on the state for income support a certainty for all but those unemployed for short spells. Current benefit levels are insufficient to maintain, even nearly, the standard of living enjoyed while at work for almost all the jobless. In these circumstances no one can be surprised at the evidence of increasing ill-health among the unemployed. The central position that work and earning occupies in an economy and culture like the UK's means that feelings of worthlessness and isolation will intensify as one week's unemployment becomes a month and then a year. The increasing individualisation of unemployment, in the sense that you are held responsible for your own jobless predicament, only serves to undermine any sense of self-esteem that has been preserved. As an unemployed person you are bombarded daily with the news that you are a scrounger and a wastrel. Senior Conservative politicians emphasise that your jobless plight is of your own making, and that the solution is in your own hands. But that they care, truly.

In the late 1980s there is no doubt that in terms of poverty, physical and mental health and social and economic deprivation 'unemployment is a corrosive experience for most people', (Charter for Jobs). When the monthly unemployment count is reported and applause is heard (when they fall) or commiserations and excuses are offered (when they rise), behind each of those seven digits of millions and thousands and hundreds there are people. These are families with children, couples, single men and women, all suffering this corrosive experience. For them unemployment is 100 per cent, and they are living through a time when, 'For the 87 per cent in work, the country has never had as good a time as it has today' (Lord Young). We should be ashamed.

6. We Are Not Alone

The increase in unemployment since 1979 is not, of course, a peculiarly British phenomenon. Other developed countries too have experienced a rise in unemployment, reaching unprecedented post-war heights in the majority of cases. However, the 1980s have seen enormous differences in unemployment in different countries. The smaller and more centrally planned economies with special characteristics have tended to fare rather better than the larger, open-trade, market-orientated economies. Japan, of course, as always, is a rather special case, with its emphasis on innovation and the continued adoption of what could politely be called aggressive international trade policies.

Virtually all countries, then, can be characterised by rising unemployment from 1979 to the mid-1980s. The steep increase in oil prices in the late 1970s and the onset of the world recession helps to explain this increase. However, in the UK the adoption of particular anti-inflation policies meant that this country stole a march on many other countries in the unemployment league. Unemployment in the UK rose faster and reached higher levels more quickly than in many comparable countries, before settling down at a real level of over 4 million. Other countries have caught up somewhat; others have attempted to stem the tide of unemployment through a variety of anti-unemployment measures (e.g. France). Others, sometimes more through accident than

Table 6.1: Unemployment rates in selected countries, (national definitions)

Country	Number unemployed 1987	Unemployment rate %
Australia[b]	634,000	8.2
Austria[b]	141,000	4.8
Belgium[b]	432,000	15.8
Canada[a]	1,142,000	8.5
Denmark[d]	248,000	9.1
France[b]	2,522,000	10.8
Germany (Fed. Rep.)[a]	2,097,000	7.4
Greece[c]	116,000	6.3
Irish Republic[a]	247,000	19.3
Italy[c]	3,353,000	14.6
Japan[e]	1,860,000	3.1
Netherlands[d]	692,000	14.2
Norway[c]	31,100	1.9
Spain[c]	2,946,000	21.2
Sweden[d]	94,000	2.1
Switzerland[d]	23,600	0.8
United Kingdom[a]	2,905,000	10.5
United States[a]	7,655,000	6.3

Notes: The figures are not directly comparable, owing to national differences.
a. June 1987. b. May 1987. c. April 1987. d. March 1987.
e. February 1987.
Source: *Employment Gazette*, August 1987.

design, have experienced substantial drops in unemployment (e.g. the USA). Still others have remained relatively unaffected by unemployment (e.g. Japan and Sweden). Table 6.1 shows the unemployment rate in a number of countries.

As with almost all information that compares countries, there are great dangers in a simple interpretation of the unemployment rates in Table 6.1. These unemployment figures reflect differences in how the statistics are compiled, the welfare-benefits systems and even, in part, the different cultures of the countries. To immerse oneself seriously in international comparisons of this kind a proper appreciation of all of these differences is required. For the time being the information contained in Table 6.1 gives us an appropriate flavour of national differences. The discussion later in this chapter on Australia, the Federal Republic of Germany and the USA assists in getting beyond the simple unemployment-rate statistics.

While the Conservative government was correct in its 1985 White Paper in stating that rising unemployment was not simply a British problem, it does need to explain just why the advance of unemployment was so fast and to such a high level in the UK. The Conservative government's policies explain our experiences. In 1979, the excess of UK unemployment over the average for the seven big industrialised countries of the Organisation for Economic Cooperation and Development (OECD) was just 0.1 per cent. In 1980 it was 0.9 per cent, before leaping up to 3.4 per cent in 1981 and 3.5 per cent in 1982. Since 1984 this excess rate of unemployment in the UK over the big-seven average has been more than 5 per cent.

Year by year during the 1980s, unemployment in the UK has worsened relative to the other large industrialised countries. While great claims are being made at home for the dips in unemployment officially recorded during 1987, especially at the time of the General Election, the waste of unemployment remains intense. There may well be some lessons that the UK can learn from the experiences of other industrialised countries. The rest of this chapter attempts to map out some of the initiatives being taken elsewhere to alleviate unemployment and considers their success or failure. It then discusses youth unemployment as a special case. For all countries, high youth unemployment is a disturbing feature of 1980s labour markets. The UK too, especially through the Youth Training Scheme and the job-subsidising New Workers Scheme (see Chapter 7), has had the young unemployed in its sights. But for male heads of household in the 25–54 age group, government initiatives have been limp. And Britain's unemployment rate for this group is nearly double that of other large industrialised countries. Perhaps a closer scrutiny of their actions for jobs can assist in this country.

AUSTRALIA

Australia is often held up these days as an example of a country where economic and social policies, held in such high esteem elsewhere in the 1960s and early 1970s, went drastically wrong in the 1980s. Australia was particularly severely hit by the first massive oil-price increase leading to deep recession. The second 'oil-shock' recession exacerbated matters, and tumbling commodity prices in the 1980s have led to a sharp economic decline. Even so, unemployment in Australia at just over 8 per cent is still lower than in the UK.

The Australian economy is nowhere near as large as that of the 'big-seven' OECD countries (Canada, France, Federal Republic of Germany, Italy, Japan, UK and the USA). Even so, it has a labour force 7 million strong, which over the decade to 1984 was growing at between 1 and 2 per cent a year. In 1985 the labour force grew by 2.3 per cent, employment outstripping this with a growth of over 3 per cent.

Manufacturing industry accounts for 20 per cent of total employment, a figure similar to the UK. Employment in manufacturing has been declining steadily, again analagous to the UK. The agricultural and mineral sectors of the economy employ 5 per cent of the labour force (while providing 40 per cent of exports, thus accounting for some of the vulnerability of the Australian economy to commodity-price changes). The service sector of the labour market accounts for 70 per cent of employment. So, while the labour force has a strength just one-third of that of the UK, the proportions employed in the different sectors are broadly similar.

In the period from 1945 until the early 1970s, the Australian economy could only be described as buoyant. It was rare indeed for the unemployment rate to go beyond 1.5 per cent. Even up until 1973 it still remained at or below 2 per cent. Then the most severe recession in Australia since the 1930s struck, increasing unemployment from 2.4 per cent in 1974 to 4.6 per cent in 1975. It peaked (for the 1970s) at 6.2 per cent in 1978, before dropping back to below 6 per cent for the following three years. A further sharp downturn occurred in 1982, boosting unemployment once again to 6.7 per cent in that year and 9.9 per cent in 1983. Economic growth in the mid-1980s has enabled Australia to generate jobs, with employment growth in 1984 and 1985 exceeding 3 per cent each year. Unemployment for 1985–7 has hovered at about the 8 per cent mark. As in the UK, the official unemployment rate (which is based on labour-force surveys *not* registered employed) is an underestimate. If all those seeking work are included then the 1987 unemployment level in Australia would be more like 15 per cent.

Figure 6.1 shows the changing unemployment rate in Australia from 1974 to 1987. It should be remembered that this has to be compared with an average rate in the late 1960s of just 1.5 per cent. The unemployment rate itself is not the only significant change that has taken place. As in the UK, the length of time the unemployed have been taking to find work has also lengthened. The average duration of unemployment in 1974 was 6.5 weeks. This increased until by 1979 the average figure was over 28 weeks. From 1983 to 1985 the average duration of unemployment was over 45 weeks, and in 1986 approached 50 weeks. It was a combination of rising unemployment rates and the lengthening duration of unemployment that led to the development of a myriad of special measures aimed at the unemployed. Because of the especially high unemployment rates among particularly disadvantaged groups, a number of these schemes have special target groups in mind. As noted in Chapter 5, it is important to know just who are the most

Figure 6.1: Unemployment percentage rates in Australia, 1974–87

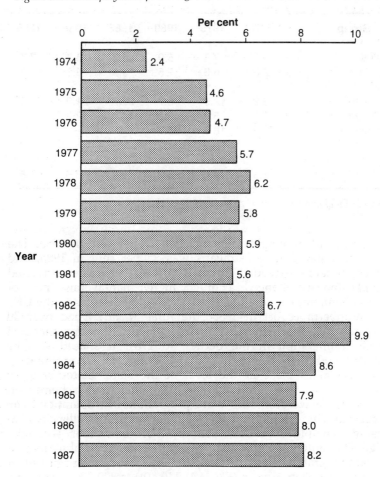

Source: *Employment Gazette*, August 1987.

at-risk groups, before embarking on unemployment-alleviation measures. For many of the Australian initiatives, this kind of thinking has been very much to the fore. Certainly, the kinds of problems facing the UK in relation to high youth unemployment, unemployment in the ethnic minorities, regional imbalances and the long-term unemployed are ones very familiar to Australian policy-makers. As Table 6.2 shows, taken from a special article on the Australian labour market in the August 1987 *Employment*

Table 6.2: Unemployment rates in Australia: special groups

Group	1970	1975	1980	1983	1984	1985
Males	1.0	3.5	5.0	9.9	8.7	7.7
Females	2.3	6.5	7.5	9.9	8.3	7.9
Young people:						
15–19	3.2	12.9	16.7	22.6	21.0	18.6
20–24	1.6	5.9	8.8	14.7	12.5	10.9
Aboriginals	9.3	18.8	24.7	–	–	–
Disabled	–	–	12.2	–	–	–
All unemployed	1.4	4.6	5.9	9.9	8.6	7.8

Source: *Employment Gazette*, August 1987.

Gazette, youth unemployment reached 23 per cent in 1983. The figure for aboriginal Australians was 25 per cent in 1980, and almost certainly exceeded 40 per cent three years later. Disabled people too experienced a much higher-than-average rate of unemployment, echoing the experience of the disabled in the UK.

A Canberra report in 1985, the *Kirby Report*, listed over 30 Commonwealth schemes for unemployment alleviation that had been in operation in the decade to 1984. It should also be remembered that, rather like the USA, much government in Australia takes place at the level of the state. States such as Queensland or New South Wales have their own schemes: in 1983–4 there were 57 such state programmes in operation. The biggest and most important special initiatives in Australia aimed at easing unemployment are listed in Table 6.3, along with any eligibility criteria employed. Special Commonwealth labour-market programmes (i.e. Federal) are now costing over 500 million Australian dollars a year (£1 = A\$2.2). Over 300,000 people are assisted by these labour-market programmes. An additional 600,000 receive unemployment benefit. So, the ratio of Commonwealth-programme participants to unemployed claimants is as low as one to two. (There are, in addition, state schemes, as noted above.) In the UK the ratio of the unemployed on special schemes to unemployed claimants is more like one to five in total.

The Regional Employment Development Scheme (REDS) was basically used as a public-sector job-creation scheme in the 1970s. REDS funded labour-intensive projects of use to the community in areas of high unemployment. The scheme was ended by the 1975 Budget. The Whitlam government also introduced the National Employment and Training System (NEAT) in order to encourage the skills acquisition of the unemployed or those at the greatest risk

Table 6.3: Australian labour-market programme

Scheme	Eligibility	Special emphasis
Regional Employment Development Scheme (REDS)	Registered unemployed	High unemployment regions Women Aboriginals
National Employment and Training System (NEAT)	Occupations in demand. Extended to unemployed	—
Special Youth Employment Training Programme (SYETP)	Teenagers unemployed for 4 months or more. Extended to 18–24-year-olds.	—
Community Youth Support Scheme (CYSS)	Unemployed under the age of 25	—
Commonwealth Rebate for Apprentice Full-time Training (CRAFT)	Employers of eligible apprentices	—
Work Pause Programme (WPP)	Young unemployed and older unemployed and disadvantaged in equal numbers. Equal numbers of men and women	Long-term unemployed Disabled Aboriginals Migrants
Community Employment Programme (CEP)	Registered unemployed for longer than 3 months	Long-term unemployed Disabled Aboriginals

Source: *Employment Gazette*, August 1987.

of becoming unemployed. In the 1980s the rump of the system remaining pays unemployment benefit plus a training allowance to those on off-the-job courses that offer opportunities for employment on completion. On-the-job subsidies can also be paid in certain circumstances. In the UK the Job Training Scheme is much meaner than this, paying only unemployment benefit to participants, with no training-allowance supplement.

The aptly named CRAFT (Commonwealth Rebate for Apprentice Full-time Training) started in the late 1970s. Under the scheme, employers receive a rebate where apprentices attend a trade school. In Australia about one in five of all school leavers still enters employment through the apprenticeship training route (one-third of male school-leavers). Creigh has estimated that up to 45 per cent of total apprenticeship costs are being met from the public-sector purse.

Youth unemployment in Australia has received a great deal of attention from policy-makers and politicians. With over one in five of those aged under 20 years old out of work at times in the 1980s, youth unemployment has been regarded as a rather special social and economic problem, as it has in most other developed countries. The Special Youth Employment Training Programme was introduced in the mid-1970s in order to assist unemployed school-leavers for six months (later reduced in time but extended in age range). The employer received the subsidy. The number of young people participating at the height of the scheme in 1978 was equivalent to one-third of unemployed 15- to 17-year-olds.

The Wage Pause Programme (WPP) was started in 1983 and received its name from the one-year wages increase 'stop' imposed on Commonwealth employees. The money thus saved was directed towards public-sector job-creation. In the fifteen months to June 1984 22,000 jobs were created with the A$200 million saved. The WPP was the first scheme since the abolition of REDS in 1975 to explicitly aim at public-sector job-creation. The 4000 projects run in the states through WPP, aimed to recruit the long-term unemployed (defined as eight months or longer) and aboriginals and migrant workers with language problems. The jobs created lasted six months on average. A third job-creation scheme was launched in 1983, when Australian unemployment was at its peak level of 10 per cent overall. The Community Employment Programme aimed to provide 40,000 jobs a year for each of three years. The main aim was to assist those groups most disadvantaged in the Australian labour market—the disabled, aboriginals and the long-term unemployed.

In 1985 Canberra published the report of a thoroughgoing review of Australian labour-market programmes, the Kirby Committee's report. A year of training for 16- and 17-year-olds through the Australian Traineeships Scheme was proposed and accepted. Like the UK's original one-year Youth Training Scheme, 13 weeks off-the-job training was required. Pilot arrangements for 1985–6 laid down a minimum wage of A$90 a week. A fee is paid to trainers and employers to cover training costs. In 1986, again following the recommendations of Kirby, a Jobstart scheme, was introduced, replacing seven existing schemes (including the SYETP). Subsidies for employment were to be 'attached' to disadvantaged individuals rather than to jobs, as a means of encouraging employers to hire them.

In terms of the success of these different measures and special schemes in evidence is patchy. Surveys of employers showed that in the Special Youth Employment Training Programme, where employers received a subsidy for providing training and work experience, up to 80 per cent of the places provided displaced other young recruits. The net addition to employment was only put at between 20 and 30 per cent. As we shall see in Chapter 7, for the UK's Young Worker's Scheme, which paid a subsidy to employers for recruiting young people to low-paid jobs, the addition to employment was put at just 16 per cent, according to an evaluation from the Institute of Manpower Studies. This means that for every 100 jobs 'created' by the Young Workers Scheme, just 16 represented new employment. For the rest, subsidies were awarded for low-paid jobs that would have existed anyway (deadweight), or young people were recruited to jobs that in the absence of a subsidy would have gone to older workers (substitution). This is always a danger when subsidies of this kind are attached to jobs rather than to the individuals seeking work. Pursuing this latter course, however, as in Australian Jobstart, does not remove these problems altogether. This being said, the evidence was that two-thirds of those on SYETP did have jobs six months after the subsidy ended. On the Work Pause Programme, over 60 per cent of participants were in full-time work a year after their WPP stint ended. The evidence from Australia seems to be that participation on a job-creation scheme can significantly improve the employment prospects of the unemployed, especially for disadvantaged groups like the long-term unemployed.

In 1987 unemployment in Australia is starting to rise again. It is planned that spending on the Community Employment Programme should fall (the public-sector job-creation programme), but that spending on vocational training measures should rise. Jobstart subsidy payments will also be increasing. In Australia, then, it would appear that increasing emphasis is now being given to labour-market supply-side initiatives—improving the quality of labour, and reducing its costs to employers. Direct intervention in the form of public-sector job expansion is becoming less important.

UNITED STATES OF AMERICA

In June 1987 unemployment in the USA was 6.3 per cent of the civilian labour force. In 1979 it was 5.8 per cent, and 1979 was the only time since 1974 that unemployment had been below 6 per cent. In 1987 unemployment in the USA was the lowest at any time in the past seven years: by the autumn of 1987 it had fallen to below 6 per cent. Figure 6.2 shows the trend in unemployment since the 1970s.

The USA did experience rising unemployment in the early 1980s, reaching 10 per cent in 1982. It remained at about this level in 1983 before moving sharply into reverse from 1984 to 1987. The USA has an unemployment rate that is the envy of the UK and a number of other countries as well. While the scale of job-creation and unemployment reduction is no longer as dramatic as in 1983–4, the gains are impressive. In that year, 6 million jobs were created,

Figure 6.2: Unemployment as a percentage of the civilian labour force in the USA, 1970–87

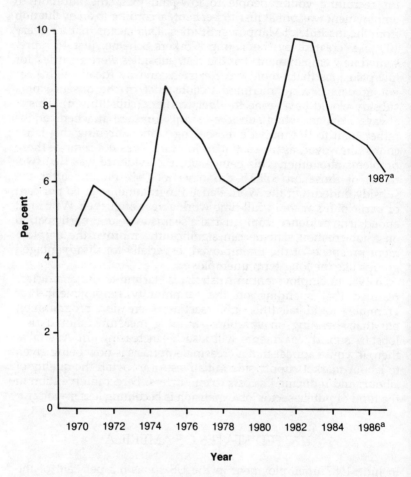

Note: a. June 1987: 6.3 per cent.
Source: Bureau of Labor Statistics.

and in a single month, October 1983, no less than three-quarters of a million unemployed Americans found work. The gains in 1987 are substantial, nevertheless.

In February 1987, 236,000 jobs were created in the USA. In March, when unemployment fell to 6.6 per cent, 165,000 new jobs were created. Listed unemployment in March fell by over 100,000. Strong increases in employment in the retail trade and in health and business services were partly undermined by further declines in manufacturing and construction employment. In April the number of jobs grew by over 300,000, resulting in a further trimming of the ranks of the unemployed. Particularly encouraging was the way a revival had started in manufacturing employment. In fact, the USA has now created over 9 million new jobs since 1983. It is important to try and understand just how this has been achieved, and whether the UK can learn anything from the American experience.

In the USA, as in the UK and Australia, unemployment has not afflicted all groups equally. Youth employment is a particular problem, and in the USA teenagers formed 23 per cent of all unemployed people in 1982, falling back now to about 18 per cent. In the USA the 'baby boom' generations of the 1960s and 1970s have been reaching working age in the 1980s, so labour supply has been increasing at a time (in the earlier 1980s) when jobs were being lost on a large scale. Labour-force growth overall has now slowed to 1.5 per cent a year. This growth is partly fuelled by new young entrants but mainly by adult women seeking work. Pat Choate has forecast that women will represent two out of every three entrants to the US labour force in the years to 1995—a million women a year.

As in the UK, those working in manufacturing, construction and the primary industries have been hardest hit by unemployment. Unemployment rates among 'blue-collar' workers have been three times higher than 'white collar' workers. The USA also has a regional problem.

When reference is made in the US literature to disadvantaged groups, while there is consideration of those in particularly hard-hit regions, the unskilled and semi-skilled 'blue-collar' workers, and those from declining industries, rather more attention is paid to the different ethnic groupings. As in the UK (see Chapter 5), black men and women experience a much higher level of unemployment than their white counterparts. Table 6.4 shows the uneven pattern of unemployment amongst the black and white populations. Black teenagers suffer the highest unemployment of all. Race discrimination again plays a large part in accounting for these differences.

While the long-term unemployed are often included among the disadvantaged groups for whom special initiatives are organised, unemployment of a year or more's duration is much less common in the USA than in the UK. In the 1982 recession, one-third of the UK's registered unemployed had been out of work for a year or more. The figure for the USA was just 8 per cent. The fluidity and flexibility of the US labour market does partly account for this difference. Sacking people is more common in the USA as a response to temporary short-term employer difficulties. Labour mobility is higher. Unemployment insurance and (after six

Table 6.4: Percentage unemployment rates among black and white groups, USA, 1985

Group	Unemployment rate %	
	All ages (16 and over)	Age 16–17 years
All men	6.2	19.1
All women	7.7	19.9
White men	5.3	15.9
White women	6.6	16.6
Black men	14.6	44.0
Black women	15.7	51.0

Source: US Bureau of Labor Statistics.

months) welfare are less generous and much more restrictive in eligibility.

It can be seen that the USA has had unemployment difficulties of some severity to deal with in the 1980s. The response has been manifold, encompassing macro-economic policy measures as well as labour-market intervention. It is just not the case that a *laissez-faire* attitude to both the economy and the labour market produced those 9 million extra jobs through the hidden hand of the market. It is wishful thinking in the UK to minimise the influence of special schemes: they do exist at federal and state levels and are at times effective. Of much greater influence, however, has been the stance adopted towards economic policy-making in the USA.

President Reagan, in a speech to the nation in 1982, commented:

> You cannot solve unemployment without solving the things that caused it—out of control inflation and interest rates that led to unemployment in the first place. Unless you get at the root cause of the problem you may be able to temporarily relieve the symptoms but you'll never cure the disease.

Consistently, in their words, President Reagan and his Administration have nailed their policies firmly to the mast of monetarism. Reaganomics on the other side of the Atlantic and Thatcherism in the UK, in the words of their arch-proponents, have apparently much in common. But the words and the policies pursued in the USA do not match well. In the UK, the American success in job-creation is explained in terms of 'vigorous economic growth and a flexible labour market' (*Employment: The Challenge for the Nation*). A free market for labour, and freer markets for goods and services are said to typify the American way and the Reagan Administration's approach to unemployment.

The prevailing wisdom in the UK is that non-intervention in the labour market is the name of the game in the USA. However, local and small-scale initiatives, particularly at the state level, are common, especially with the aim of assisting disadvantaged groups, such as the long-term unemployed or those in the inner cities. One quite large programme is derived from the Job Training Partnership Act, where training and assistance in job placements are given to the young unemployed and the long-term jobless. 'Workfare' schemes are commonplace, where the unemployed do jobs that are of 'community value' in return for welfare payments. There are other initiatives, some of which are discussed below.

A stepwise change in US economic and social policy was expected with the arrival of Ronald Reagan in the White House. At first, Reagan resisted pressures to solve or ameliorate rising unemployment. The preference was for making monetary and labour markets work better. Budget cuts in social-expenditure programmes together with substantial tax reductions were expected to stimulate economic activity through consumption and investment increases, thus *indirectly* creating jobs. As the quote above indicates, lower government spending, lower interest rates and lower taxation would provoke the market response to unemployment. But with over 10 million unemployed in 1983, the Reagan Administration resolve on labour market intervention weakened.

The Job Training Partnership Act provided for vocational skills training for the low-income unemployed. The Act also gave more power to state and county governments in running programmes. National Job Corps were established to educate and train disadvantaged young people. The Job Corps is the only nationwide intensive education and vocational-skills programme for young people. In comparison with something like the YTS (see Chapter 7) its size is puny—just over 40,000 places. Other projects aimed at young people include the Youth Incentive Entitlement Pilot Project (YIEPP) aimed at those in secondary education who may drop out before completing their studies. The American Conservation Corps (ACC) aims to create 100,000 jobs for unemployed and disadvantaged young people refurbishing parks and forests. In 1983 the Reagan Administration made its own unemployment alleviation proposals with a $5.4-billion package aimed at creating a minimum 3 million jobs in 1983 and 1984. The package included retraining opportunities for the unemployed. Entitlement to unemployment benefit was extended from six months to a year to assist those who, in very · difficult labour-market conditions, had run out of unemployment insurance benefits, and were relying increasingly on welfare. A Jobs Tax Credit reimbursed employers part (or all) of the wages of disadvantaged workers who were recruited. About 2 million jobs a year are held by young people whose employers are assisted in this way.

Resources for such schemes are relatively scarce, however. It has been estimated that the amount of money available under the Job Training Partnership Act is only sufficient to provide training for just 4 per cent of the eligible population. Because of the scale of the unemployment problem in 1982–3, many states filled the federal void by launching their own training and job-creation initiatives. Wage subsidies are available in many states to employers who increase their headcount, especially where those recruited are long-term unemployed or belong to other disadvantaged groups. Other states (at least 22 of them) are encouraging high/new technology industries to locate or relocate within their borders. Compensation is now more commonly available to those workers required to shift to part-week working. The trade unions too have been trying to assist by providing funds for the retraining of 'displaced' members (e.g. United Auto Workers) and in other ways.

So, at federal, state and local levels, there is in existence a range of unemployment-alleviation and training and retraining measures. They have certainly helped in the turnaround but, frankly, have been of minor importance and have not contributed massively to the American job-generation machine of the past three years. What really has made the difference, and where the USA and UK deviate sharply, is in their pursuit of national economic policies.

The Reagan economic objectives in 1981 to curb inflation, improve productivity, reduce public spending, cut taxes and cut unemployment were similar to those of the first Thatcher government in 1979. The Reagan strategy for achieving these aims has been described by Sawhill and Palmer as an, 'unconventional mixture of monetary directives and untested supply side theories'. In fact, and in the event, inflation was reduced (world factors played a major part in this in the USA as in the UK), income taxes were reduced, public spending was *increased*, not cut, and a huge deficit between spending and revenue resulted, and unemployment rose and fell. The labour-market and general economic recovery in the USA was described by *Businessweek* in 1984 as, 'less like a supply-side miracle than an old fashioned super Keynesian expansion'.

Traditional Keynesian-type stand-by policies (see Chapter 2) of budget deficits and tax cuts stimulated the US economy to generate jobs. Six million jobs in 18 months was the great achievement: over 9 million in four years. These jobs were *not* created by adherence to monetarist dogma, or supply-side policies but by a super (and imprudently sized) Keynesian-style reflation of the economy. Spending your way out of recession still can work in the 1980s, or so the US experience would indicate.

The expansion in the USA that began in 1982 has been a conventional demand-led recovery on a grand scale fuelled by huge deficit-spending policies. But what deficits! The budget deficit rose from $10 billion in early 1981 to $62 billion by early 1982, and to $180 billion in the fourth quarter of 1982. It has remained at these sorts of level — $200 billion in 1986 was the excess of government spending over revenue received, mainly through taxation. This has provided a massive fiscal boost to the economy. This is all very curious in a country that exported unreconstituted monetarism to the UK, and with a Reagan Administration that in its own words has been committed to the Thatcher way.

There are other notable features of the US experience in the 1980s. Contrary to the still-heard (but less frequent) rhetoric emanating from Downing Street, a rise in money supply has *not* led to rapidly rising inflation. Indeed, if the UK government believed its medium-term financial-strategy statements from the early 1980s, with the then-favoured money-supply definition M3 (there are lots) growing in 1987 at over 20 per cent a year, we really would have every reason to fear high inflation in the near future. It did not happen in the USA that money-supply growth fuelled inflation, and it will not happen in the UK.

Private-sector spending in the USA has not been 'crowded out' by high public expenditure. There is this popular notion that money, resources or people used in the public services prevent the productive, marketable sectors of the economy (i.e. profit-making but not in public ownership) from thriving. This is the flat-Earth theory of how the economy works. The economy is viewed as a ruler: four inches in the public services cannot be used for anything else. This is a nonsense. Rather, the economy is like a rubber band, expanding then contracting, but certainly in a circle. The public sector places orders with private-sector companies (where does education get its books, or computers, or the health service its drugs?); those in receipt of unemployment or supplementary benefit spend it. And unlike those in work with higher incomes, and perhaps receiving tax cuts, they will typically spend it on home-produced goods and services rather than imports. Instead of high public spending 'crowding out' or inhibiting the development of private enterprise, the reverse can and does happen. Public spending can stimulate private-economy activity. Certainly in the USA in the 1980s, the private sector has expanded along with government spending.

The costs that were paid for the expansionist US policies up until the autumn of 1987 were continuing high interest rates and some confusion in the currency markets. However, the world stock-market crash in October 1987 was a direct result of the Reagan Administration's continuing failure to direct its attention to the $200-billion gap between government revenue and its spending, and its failure to address the imbalance between exports and imports (the trade deficit). Budget deficits have had an enormous job-creating and stimulating effect on the US economy. But the scale of the deficit, and the reluctance of Reagan and his advisors to prune their ambitions on income tax cuts and defence spending, led to the crash. Increased taxes on the better off and early action on defence spending (growing by 10 per cent a year in the 1980s), particularly on 'Star Wars', could have staved off the undermining of confidence so apparent in October 1987. The penalties that are likely to be paid worldwide for such inaction are unemployment rising even higher, and the labelling of even prudent budget deficits as potentially catastrophic.

The US labour market is more flexible than that of the UK. Competition generally is more intense, and internal competition fiercely guarded (trade barriers are another matter). But there have been, and are, a range of special measures aimed at training, retraining and job-creation for the unemployed. However, neither flexibility nor special schemes account for the enormous achievements in the USA of cutting unemployment from 10 per cent to under 6 per cent in four years, with the creation of millions of jobs. Disadvantaged groups still experience very high unemployment. There remains a regional problem. But the success there has been achieved, rather unwillingly by the Republican Administration, and perhaps unwittingly by Reagan himself, by a rather large overdose of Keynesian medicine. Continuing high government spending, tax cuts, and a large divergence between government spending and revenue have provided the stimulation for the US economy to create jobs and cut unemployment. The pace has been too quick and the deficit far too large, but there is certainly a lesson here for the UK.

FEDERAL REPUBLIC OF GERMANY

In 1983, when registered unemployment in the UK stood at 3.1 million, the figure in the Federal Republic of Germany (FRG) was 2.3 million. In the FRG it stayed at the 2.3 million mark (annual average) for the following three years. For 1987 too the average figure for the year was in excess of 2 million. The 7.4 per cent unemployment rate in June 1987 represented 2.1 million people. The figure for June 1986 was identical. The 7.4 per cent rate is calculated as a percentage of total employees: it is about 9 per cent of the working population.

The FRG started the 1950s with an unemployment rate in excess of 10 per cent. Unemployment then steadily fell until by 1961 it had reached just under 1 per cent. Full employment (at an unemployment level of 2 per cent or less) was then the experience until the early 1970s. A reasserted commitment to full-employment policies, together with a re-alignment in West German politics, took place following the 2 per cent unemployment rate of 1966–7. Unemployment was halved in the following two years.

In common with most other industrialised countries, the 1973 oil-price shock caused a substantial increase in unemployment in the mid-1970s. From 1975 to 1977 over 1 million were out of work. With the prudent use of public-expenditure increases a million new jobs were created in the FRG in the four years to 1980: unemployment had been cut to less than 900,000 (labour supply was still growing at this time).

From the second oil-price shock unemployment rose to 1.8 million in 1982 and, as stated above, 2.3 million thereafter. These still-higher levels of unemployment were experienced despite a commitment on the part on the incoming 'Conservative' Kohl government in 1982 that unemployment would and could be reduced to 1 million by 1985. Jobs have been created, with over half a million more people in work in 1987 than three years previously. But more jobs than this were required just to stand still. And, as in the UK, the official count of the unemployed does not include many of those out of work and looking for a job. In the FRG's case, it is estimated by Charter for Jobs that this group amounts to an additional 1 million unemployed people.

The FRG also has a regional problem, with regional variations in unemployment growing rather than diminishing. It also has an ethnic problem, although in the FRG it is frequently not described in such terms. The recruitment of workers from abroad in the 1960s and 1970s to meet labour bottlenecks in production, has been thrust in reverse. In 1973, one in ten employees was a foreign worker. By 1986 this figure had fallen to 6 per cent. The reversal of *Gästarbeiter* (literally: guest worker) encouragement has at times produced overtly racist and discriminatory proposals.

Chancellor Kohl had intended to cut unemployment through the use of 'supply-side' policies. They have not been successful. The UK's Conservative government interprets the Kohl aims as a firm belief that the remedy for high unemployment lies (once again) in the 'better working of markets', in particular making the labour market more flexible. We are authoritatively told by the Thatcher government that the Germans in the FRG have no large programmes aimed at reducing unemployment directly. This is somewhat at odds with the *fact* that currently over 400,000 West German employees have jobs or are in training because of special labour-market schemes. Spending on labour-market measures doubled in the three years to 1986, and now cost over 9 billion Deutschmarks a year.

The FRG also has a much respected extensive system of vocational training for young people, developed to meet skill needs during the good times. This is rather different from the knee-jerk immediacy of the YTS (see Chapter 7), cobbled together speedily in response to high youth unemployment. On average, over two years' training—both on and off the job—are provided for 1.7 million new entrants to work each year.

One should also take note of the drive towards a shorter working week in the FRG. The aim is to achieve a 35-hour working week, with time being knocked off in stages. There is potential here for unemployment alleviation, too. There have been moves to increase the 'flexibility' of the labour market in the FRG, mainly by eroding the right of employees in work, particularly affecting part-time and short-term contract workers and women.

One of the leading supply-siders in the UK, Patrick Minford, gives great emphasis to his policy of limiting unemployment benefit to some proportion of previous take-home pay. This is already done in the FRG, with the effect that a German in receipt of unemployment benefit (not all are eligible) is on average much better-off than the unemployed Briton. Employers and employees contribute to unemployment insurance, and the benefits received vary from 63 to 68 per cent of previous take-home pay, depending on circumstances (number of dependants etc). These insurance payments can last up to 32 months before the unemployed become dependent on what the Americans would call welfare. These means-tested benefits, for those still eligible, pay from 56 to 58 per cent of last net income while at work. Unless a very low maximum possible benefit level were set, there is no evidence from the FRG that relating benefit to previous pay would produce the massive gains to employment forecast by Minford.

The Federal Republic's economy in the 1980s has stuck on a plateau of unemployment. The real level of unemployment is almost certainly over 3 million. Special schemes for the unemployed do make a contribution to unemployment alleviation: supply-side measures, other than to attempt to shift the balance of power in the labour market towards employers and away from workers and their trade unions have been fairly impotent. The FRG economy has benefited from external factors more recently (as has the UK). Growing export demand, particularly in the USA and newly falling oil and other commodity prices have certainly helped. Some of the prospects for the later 1980s, particularly for the unemployed, are less good.

Bankers are not renowned for their spendthrift natures. But Dr Nolling, President of the Federal Reserve Bank of Hamburg, has argued that the government of the FRG should stimulate demand in order to reduce unemployment, through a combination of higher-targeted public spending and cuts in taxation. He has also argued that consideration should be given to providing all 600,000 of those unemployed for a year or longer with a government-subsidised job or a place on a training programme. The net cost of such a programme would be 9 billion Deutschmarks or £3 billion. In the absence of changes and the adoption of proposals of this kind, Dr Nolling feels that there are good reasons for thinking that unemployment in the FRG will continue to increase. In his lecture, published by Charter for Jobs in 1987, Dr Nolling's concluding comments should strike a chord with all those concerned about the crisis of unemployment, whatever their nationality:

> Although the German system of unemployment compensation takes care of the basic financial needs of the unemployed, it should not be overlooked that there remains economic hardship and deprivation, especially among families with children and the long-term unemployed. In addition, the many negative human aspects of unemployment need to be stressed again: the social deprivation, the loss of self-esteem, the hopelessness among young people, the feeling of not being wanted any more. Western Societies should not submit to a situation where the demands and aspirations of an ever-increasing segment are ignored.

This is as true for Munich as it is for Memphis, Melbourne, or Manchester.

YOUTH UNEMPLOYMENT

Australia, the USA and the Federal Republic of Germany all have a disproportionate number of their young people out of work. The same is true for the UK, Ireland, Italy, France and the Netherlands. Towards the end of the 1970s most countries had a marked increase in youth unemployment over the beginning of the decade. Although there were some instances of stabilisation, and in fewer cases an improvement over a few years earlier, in the European Community as a whole the youth unemployment rate stood at 10 per cent. Since the late 1970s the situation has become much, much worse. With the exception of the FRG, youth unemployment rates in the main are some three times higher than that for the labour market generally.

One of the main reasons for such high youth unemployment is simply accident of birth or poor timing on the part of the young people themselves! In any recession it is the new entrants to the labour market that tend to suffer first and worst. In an early response to trading difficulties employing organisations tend to stop recruiting. There is a particular problem here for young school-leavers, who are relatively unskilled and perhaps with few or no qualifications. Graduates (also new entrants) tend to feel the effects of recession later and less severely, because most companies will build their graduate requirements into manpower plans that allow for management succession. Graduates also feel the benefits of any upturn early and strongly.

Young new entrants to the labour market, then, will feel the effects of recession and employer behaviour severely and early on. This has generally been true in all industralised countries. But in the 1980s it has been the way youth unemployment has risen so quickly and to such high levels, and stayed there, that has provoked special policy responses in the countries affected. Often, policy measures have focused on the young rather than adult or the long-term unemployed, or particularly disadvantaged groups (e.g. the disabled). In the UK, there has been a very different response to the plight of the young unemployed in terms of the speed of setting up the Youth Training Scheme, the numbers of places involved and the commitment to funding in comparison with, say, the long-term unemployed. The attention to the young in most countries has a number of reasons. Partly it has been because of the very poor employment prospects of young people who have never had a job. And each year they face stiff competition from other young new entrants to the labour market. Clearly, part of the response has been influenced by a growing concern about the likely political and social consequences of bringing along a 'welfare generation' without work habits and not having imbibed the work ethic. The development of programmes for the young unemployed may have rather less to do with a genuine heartfelt concern about the plight of the young without a role or stake in society than some politicians would have us believe.

Most of the unemployment alleviation measures adopted in other countries, as in the UK, can reasonably be considered 'supply-side' measures, and have taken two main themes. First, there are education and training measures, aimed at improving the quality of the labour supply available to employers. In this category there is the YTS in the UK, the Australian Traineeships Scheme and the Job Corps in the USA. France has a YTS-type programme with over 300,000 places. And the FRG, of course, as noted above, has its own highly developed vocational and induction training system for new entrants to the labour force, although certainly *not* specifically aimed at the unemployed or those young people least likely to get jobs.

The second supply-side measure adopted concerns wage costs to employers. The aim here has been to price young people into work by offering one or more employment subsidies, national-insurance rebates, or easing minimum-wage regulations. As long ago as the 1930s, Nicholas Kaldor was persuasively arguing the case for employment subsidies from government rather than wage cuts in an attempt to encourage employers to take on more staff. Examples of the way this message has now been adopted worldwide are many, although the supply-siders have been earnestly urging wage cuts, too. (As an aside, it is a little curious how huge salary increases and income tax cuts are required as an incentive for some, whereas lower wages are required as an incentive for others!) The UK, of course, has the New Workers Scheme (see Chapter 7), which is a subsidy to employers who recruit young people on low wages. This country has some tradition of such measures, including the Recruitment Subsidy for School Leavers (RSSL) in the mid-1970s, and the Youth Employment Subsidy after that. France also has some tradition of employment subsidies for young people (and for other groups). In the past such measures have often been adopted as part of an anti-unemployment pact between the trade unions and the government. So, in the late 1970s there was the Incentive Bonus for Job Creation, providing a six-month subsidy for the hiring of an unemployed person under 25 years of age, or completing national service. Sometimes these subsidies have targeted particular regions in France. Exemptions from employer social security contributions are also available in France for the recruitment of young people. The FRG has always put much more effort and attention into training subsidies rather than attempting to cut wage costs in one way or another.

Rather more emphasis is being given in many countries these days to employment subsidies and wage cuts. The main reason for this is the belief, in the UK as elsewhere, that crudely put, many workers are pricing themselves out of jobs. This belief particularly applies to young people. As *Employment: The Challenge for the Nation* commented in 1985, 'For all these countries, high unemployment among the young is a worrying new feature. It is due partly to the general shortage of jobs, but in Britain it also reflects high relative pay . . .' There exists this conviction that the wage costs of young people are too high to permit many (most?) of them to find work. If only wages were lower in real terms, the argument runs, and if only unemployment benefits were much lower still, and if only young people had better vocational skills, then youth unemployment could be properly tackled. There are a number of difficulties with this train of argument, in whatever country they are used. If there are no jobs, there are no jobs. This is a problem of the demand for labour by employers, closely related to the demand for the goods and services that labour (young and old) produces. Employment subsidies, lowering wage expectations and general training, unless targeted towards areas where such trained staff are in demand, will make little difference to unemployment unless there is a stepwise change in the factors that influence the demand for labour. They are palliatives, hitting at symptoms and not causes, while at the same time rather usefully keeping the unemployed actively engaged in something, sometimes anything.

And rather less usefully, except for the politicians, keeping the official unemployment count down—and they certainly do that.

As noted earlier on, the UK government is poised to solve youth unemployment for 16- and 17-year-olds. The country is adopting one-half of the East European solution to unemployment, as interpreted by Yves Laulan. In 1988 the Conservative government will be declaring that there will be no more unemployed 16- and 17-year olds in the UK. It is as simple as that. Now there are sufficient YTS places for all, participation will become compulsory for all those without a job or a place in education. Failure to comply will mean failure to receive benefits. And, of course, if you are not a claimant you are no longer included in the official unemployment count. Large tick, rule off, unemployment solved for this age group! It may not produce any more jobs, and the problems for those aged 18 and over will remain, but nevertheless, it is a politically valuable manoeuvre. Expanding the Job Training Scheme (essentially training and work on benefit) to cater for all 18- to 25-year-olds, make participation compulsory, and presto, youth unemployment, and some more, disappears in a puff of blue smoke. Other countries will be watching this response to youth unemployment most carefully.

CONCLUSIONS

Lack of demand in the economies of the industrialised world explains most of the rise in unemployment that has occurred since the late 1970s: whether this was in Australia, the FRG, France, Italy, the UK or the USA. The typical policy-response has been to adopt supply-side measure to some degree, to 'improve' the workings of labour markets. Additional vocational training and retraining to improve the quality of labour, and mechanisms to make labour cheaper for employers are the two main forms such initiatives have taken. The ability of employers to hire and fire more readily has also been enhanced. And there are attempts to reduce the quantity of labour available for work. The supply-siders have also altered the balance of influence in the labour market towards employers, and away from employees and their trade union representatives. Rather than the stimulation of demand to create jobs internationally, the stance adopted has typically been one of retrenchment and, in economic perversity, deflation. This has made matters worse.

Certainly, some countries have fared better, or not as badly, as others. The enthusiasm of any particularly government for monetary deflation and public-spending cuts can account for these differences. Most, however, have intervened in the workings of their precious market for labour by introducing employment subsidies of some kind, training and retraining measures, community-project employment or just (in small part) good old-fashioned public-sector job-creation. For reasons best known to themselves, the scale of such initiatives abroad go unrecognised by HM Government. They can assist in unemployment amelioration, and the UK has been no laggard in endorsing this approach and expanding provision. A quick perusal of the *Action for Jobs* booklet is sufficient evidence for this. But it is tinkering.

In the 1980s it is the USA that has had the greatest success of any of the large economies suffering from unemployment in cutting down the numbers unemployed and in creating jobs. The evidence produced in this chapter shows that the creation of over 9 million jobs, and the cut in unemployment from 10 to 6 per cent, was achieved through expansionist public-sector spending policies and an imprudently burgeoning budget deficit. Demand-side policies have been used to counteract what is essentially a demand problem. The rhetoric of the Reagan Administration has not been matched by its actions in the economy. Income tax cuts, especially for the rich, and public-spending inreases, particularly on defence, have helped to stimulate demand and create jobs. Australia, the FRG and the UK and other countries have set their faces firmly against such a response to unemployment. The problem with the US response to policy-making has been its patent failure to ensure control and planning over its budget deficit. Corrective action taken earlier in 1987 would certainly have averted the world stock-exchange crash in October 1987. It was the scale of the imbalance between government revenue and expenditure that caused the problems, not the fact that a budget deficit existed at all. Indeed, it is now apparently the aim of the Thatcher government in 1988 to have a small surplus on the public account in the UK, after years of whittling down government borrowing. The achievement of such an aim, whereby government revenue would actually *exceed* spending, reins back attempts at job creation even further. This is the complete opposite of what should be done at a time of 4 million unemployed.

In the design of its special schemes, the UK can learn a little from those in operation in other countries, particularly when aimed at specially disadvantaged groups. The biggest lesson, which regrettably will remain unlearnt for the present, is that unemployment can only be halved or better with expansionist, demand-led policies. The years 1986 and 1987 were the good times. Unless international unemployment is put firmly in reverse now, then with the onset of the next world recession, today's economic and social problems caused by the crisis of unemployment will seem like a pleasant walk in the Black Forest.

7. Special Schemes: Cure or Con?

One of the growth industries in the UK in the 1980s has been the unemployment 'industry'. Special government measures aimed at the unemployed have been developed in abundance, and expanded greatly. This country now has a large variety of schemes, aimed at different unemployed groups. At any one time they have the effect of taking over 700,000 unemployed people out of the unemployment count. The relative sizes of the different schemes are shown in Table 7.1. There is, in addition, the Job Training Scheme (JTS), which at the time of writing was still building up its numbers. The intention has been to have over 100,000 trainees on JTS by October 1987. This scheme has faced particularly intense opposition. There are also a number of other, much smaller, special employment training and 'enterprise' measures not shown in Table 7.1.

YOUTH TRAINING SCHEME

The single largest special measure is the Youth Training Scheme. In the year to March 1988 there are expected to be over 365,000 entrants to YTS schemes. YTS replaced the shorter and much criticised Youth Opportunities Programme in 1983. As originally designed, YTS provided a year's integrated work experience and

Table 7.1: Government employment measures in Great Britain, June 1987

Special scheme	Number of participants
Youth Training Scheme	344,100
Community Industry	8,000
Community Programme	232,000
Enterprise Allowance Scheme	90,000
Job Release Scheme	22,000
Jobshare	600
Jobstart Allowance	7,000
New Workers Scheme	24,000
Total	727,700

vocational training for participants, including at least 13 weeks off-the-job training. From 1986 a two-year programme was introduced with 20 weeks off-the-job training in total. The expanded YTS can provide two years for 16-year-old and one year for 17-year-old young people. There are now sufficient places for all, which permits a 'guarantee' to be made that all young people can be catered for by the Christmas of their school-leaving year. In 1987 participation was not yet formally compulsory for unemployed young people, but it will become so in 1988. In the financial year 1985–6 YTS alone cost over £800 million.

The aim of YTS is to give young people vocational skills that will help them get permanent jobs. It is supposed to be a training for the future. We have to make a judgement about whether YTS is much more than a mechanism for reducing the unemployment count and a highly visible action to show that government cares and is at least doing something about high youth unemployment. Can it assist young people in the transition to proper jobs, and is the training really of sufficient quality to improve the skills of labour and to help in the economic revival of British industry? The evidence is patchy.

One of the most fundamental problems with YTS is with its muddy objectives. It is attempting to provide essential vocational training for young people, but simultaneously it is an explicit unemployment-alleviation measure that provides very cheap labour for employers. Unlike West Germany's vocational training programme for new entrants to the labour market, designed in the times of higher employment, YTS had some modest aims when it came to the content of the scheme. The most important aim was to get a large-scale scheme for young people off the ground as quickly as possible. It was hoped that YTS would be used by employers to meet their ordinary training needs as well as in assisting the unemployed. This has happened to some extent, but in so doing it has emasculated the traditional apprenticeship training system in the UK and, for some employers, has led to ordinary school-leaver recruitment being severely curtailed and sometimes cancelled altogether. YTS places are being offered where formerly companies would be recruiting school-leavers to jobs. YTS gives employers an opportunity to 'taste and try' potential recruits over an extended period. They will keep some on, but readily let others go. And certainly some of the outcomes 'promised' by employers for YTS trainees are surely actionable under the Trades Description Act.

It is estimated by the Manpower Services Commission (MSC) — to be renamed the Training Commission — that 15 per cent of all those leaving YTS schemes do so before actually completing their training. It is claimed as a success if young people do leave and obtain a permanent job. But if the training is of such high quality and is so necessary, as claimed by the MSC, then a failure to complete training, for whatever reason, really should be of some concern. At present up to 30,000 school-leavers not in jobs and not staying on in education, also choose not to join a YTS scheme. Of course, this choice will not be available to them for much longer, if they wish to receive benefits of some kind. No longer will young people be able to persist in what has been called 'subsidised laziness'. According to research by the British Market Research Bureau, low pay was the reason most often given by YTS 'refusniks' for their non-participation. The rather uninformative 'dislike of YTS' was most often given as a reason for early leaving. YTS trainees receive £28.50 a week during their first year and £35 in the second. This can be supplemented by their employers or scheme organisers.

As noted above, YTS is supposed to be a training for the future. The ideal would certainly reflect the changing demand for skills by employers, as well as permitting trainees to gain slots in the labour market on completion. In fact, the industrial and services distribution of places does not reflect current employment patterns of young people at all well. And there is no perspective taken on future skill needs. The main determinant of the balance of YTS places is simply the supply of places. The important thing has been to provide YTS places; how they reflect labour-market needs is another matter altogether. There is a very heavy bias towards the services, and towards certain services at that. Thirty per cent of young entrants to the labour market (with jobs) go into manufacturing. But manufacturing provides only 15 per cent of YTS places. Distribution and other services (including catering and tourism) are supplying over two-thirds of YTS places. There is also concern about the amount of sexual stereotyping that occurs with YTS placements. Of female YTS trainees, 80 per cent go to work in the retail, clerical and personal-service sectors of the labour market, a figure higher than the proportion of adult women working in these areas. Staying in these sectors can lead to poorer conditions of employment, less job security, poorer training, lower pay and a greater likelihood of seasonal or part-time work.

The question has to be repeated. Is YTS adequately preparing young people for future opportunities in the labour market? The answer has to be a resounding no. Places are accepted from whatever source; the response is 'yes please' to employers and training-scheme organisers, to almost anything they are offering. There is no labour-market perspective taken. The emphasis to date has been in securing sufficient YTS places and filling them. The individual needs of young people themselves and the longer-term skill requirements of the British economy are ignored.

In view of all this, it is rather surprising to find such high numbers of YTS-leavers finding jobs on completion. This really does say something about the motivation, adaptability and enthusiasm for work of the young people themselves. In the six-month period to March 1986, one-half of those leaving YTS found full- or part-time work (47 per cent full-time). This includes early leavers as well as those staying through to the end. It is still relatively early days for YTS, especially for the two-year option. Evaluation is taking place in a number of quarters, including internal work by the Manpower Services Commission itself. There certainly is a place for high-quality vocational training for young people supported by the state. But attempting to provide training and simultaneously pushing out what has been called a 'lifeboat' to the young unemployed, merely confuses the issues. The aim must be to provide quotas of higher-quality training places according to current and future labour-market needs. This would have proper relevance to all employing organisations, and the relevance would also be readily recognised by young people themselves. Compulsion becomes unnecessary with high-quality skills training and proper rewards for trainees. This should be the aim.

NEW WORKERS SCHEME

In June 1987, 24,000 young people in Britain held their jobs with the assistance of the New Workers Scheme (NWS). The figure for April was 34,000. According to the government brochure *Action for Jobs*, 'The New Workers Scheme is designed to help young people setting out into the world of work and to encourage employers to create more job openings'. NWS is a slightly amended version of the Young Workers Scheme (YWS) introduced in 1982. Both are a job-subsidy to employers, introduced in response to concern about young people pricing themselves out of work. For YWS the minimum eligibility age was 17. With two-year YTS covering 16- and 17-year-olds, NWS is aimed at 18- to 20-year-olds. The mechanism of the job subsidy is this: if an employer takes on a young person in his or her first year of employment (YTS does not count as employment in this), then providing the pay levels are low enough, the *employer* receives a wage subsidy. For 18- and 19-year-olds, a £15 a week subsidy is paid to the employer for a year if wages are £55 a week or less. For 20-year-olds the weekly wage limit is raised to £65.

The aim is to encourage the employment of young people by driving down wages. A particular incentive is thus offered to employers to keep wages below the £55 and £65 thresholds. It is also expected that the low levels of pay on YTS followed by higher (but still relatively low) wages with NWS support, will alter young people's wage expectations. There is the potential here to widen the earnings differential between young and older workers, thus encouraging more youth employment.

The NWS subsidy has an important, distinctive feature. It is a flow subsidy. Employers can be eligible for it whether or not their total number of employees goes up or not: they can qualify on the recruitment of a young person at the right wage level. A stock subsidy, on the other hand, would be paid only when the total number of employees increased. The other important feature is that, unlike the Jobstart Allowance (see below), the subsidy is paid to the employer and not to the employee. One concern with the NWS relates to the provision of training by the employer claiming the subsidy: there need not be any. There is no requirement that the employer carries out any training whatsoever. This has to be a mistake.

Work has been carried out to try to assess the number of new jobs created by the use of job subsidies of this kind. One of the most thoroughgoing was an evaluation of the YWS undertaken by Amin Rajan of the Institute of Manpower Studies. Rajan identified three main kinds of subsidy-induced effects on employment. First, there is the *deadweight* effect. This occurs where the subsidy is claimed by employers for jobs that would have been created in any case, whether or not a subsidy existed. Where there is substantial deadweight, employers are basically being paid to do what they would have done anyway. The second effect identified is the *substitution* effect. The substitution effect promotes the employment of the target groups, in this case young people, at the expense of other groups to whom no job subsidy is attached, e.g. older unemployed people. The substitution effect, then, brings young people into jobs rather than others, and redistributes unemployment instead of counteracting it. The third, and important, effect is the *net incremental* effect. This is the true job-creation effect, where the job subsidy actually aids the employment of young people, without displacing other workers and where the jobs would not have been created without the help of a subsidy.

In his research into YWS, Rajan found that four-fifths of the jobs 'created' by the scheme were deadweight. These were jobs that would have existed even without the subsidy. Substitution accounted for 4 per cent, with the existence of the subsidy shifting some employers' hiring preferences to young workers over the older unemployed; 16 per cent was net incremental. So, for every 100 jobs for which a YWS subsidy was received, 80 would have come about in any case, for young people and within the appropriate wage band, four jobs went to young people instead of older workers, and 16 new, additional jobs were created. The Department of Employment found one person coming off the unemployment register for every four YWS grants paid. At best this implies a 25 per cent net incremental effect, with at least the possibility of an element of substitution creeping in.

In terms of new jobs created, YWS was slightly more successful than earlier experiments with job subsidies for young people: the Recruitment Subsidy for School Leavers (1975) and the Youth Employment Subsidy (1976). But the success was still very modest. NWS will not be much different in terms of impact, and over the 1986–8 period is costing £485 million. The trade unions have warned that no new jobs would be created. This is too pessimistic, but of the 24,000 young people assisted in June 1987, just 4000 will be in additional, new jobs. It is more than nothing.

COMMUNITY INDUSTRY

This special employment measure is also aimed at young people. There are 8000 places. The scheme provides temporary employment for up to a year on socially useful projects. Examples include painting and decorating, gardening and landscaping, and acting as care assistants. The groups assisted in this way by Community Industry participants are often the elderly or the handicapped. Part of the time spent with Community Industry might be workshop-based, involving metal- or wood-working. Participants can also be involved in studying part-time simultaneously with working. The scheme is aimed at 17- to 19-year-olds with special employment problems. Community Industry has a long pedigree, having started in 1972. It cost £26 million in 1984–5.

COMMUNITY PROGRAMME

This is the second-largest special-employment measure, and has in its sights those who have been unemployed for a long time. It really is the only substantial unemployment alleviation measure for the long-term unemployed. To be eligible participants aged 25 and above have to be unemployed for at least 12 of the previous 15 months. Younger applicants should have been unemployed for at least six of the previous nine months. For disabled unemployed people a shorter duration of unemployment can make them eligible.

The Community Programme (CP) replaced the Community Enterprise Programme at the end of 1982. It aims to provide work for the unemployed on projects of benefit to the community, as its name suggests. Participants can work full- or part-time for up to a year. In June 1987 there were over 230,000 people on CP projects. Since not everybody actually does a year, the number of people on projects at some time during 1987 will exceed 300,000. There has been a rapid expansion in the number of places on schemes over the past three years—in 1985, for example, there were just 130,000 places. The extra cost of providing an additional 100,000 places between 1985 and 1986 was put at £140 million. David Metcalf (see Chapter 8) has estimated the net cost of a CP place at £2200 (1984/85).

Examples of the kind of work carried out by CP participants include, according to *Action for Jobs*,

> clearing up derelict land and canals, gardening and decorating for elderly and disabled people, adapting buildings for community use, tourism and countryside projects, setting up creches and adventure playgrounds, running city farms, insulating lofts—and many other worthwhile activities.

Those working on projects normally spending a minimum of three months and a maximum 12 months with the Community Programme. They are then back on the dole, unless they have been fortunate enough to find permanent employment in the meantime. The projects on which they work, in order to get official approval, should not otherwise have been carried out.

While 'officially' participants are paid the local rate for the job, in practice the rule that the average wage limit for any project is £67 a week means that wages paid are usually less than the going rate. What this means is that project organisers can pay some participants more than £67, but in order to do so others must receive less. The average remuneration level of £67 cannot be breached. The effect of this is to make a high proportion of CP participants part-time, allowing them to claim benefit for days when they are not involved in project work. If CP wages had been maintained in line with average earnings, the project average wage should have been £85 in 1987. CP is explicitly an unemployment-alleviation and work-experience measure. Participants are not included in the monthly unemployment count. At present projects invariably contain no training element whatsoever. This is one of the most important criticisms of the Community Programme. Other criticisms concern the rates of pay for participants, the bias in the type of community work available, and quite simply the number of places. The single most serious deficiency of CP is the lack of vocational training.

The CP is the single largest programme for long-term unemployed people, but it remains a low-skill-level, 'work'-creation special measure. In spite of the supply-side emphasis on training and retraining, and improving the quality of labour (including, presumably, that reserve army of labour which includes the unemployed), training just does not feature as being at all important. Indeed, the instructions to those contemplating or proposing new CP projects is crystal clear on the issue of training: 'As a Community Programme sponsor you will not be required to provide training'. If the sponsor does wish to provide training for those working on his particular project, then the training has to relate closely to the actual work being carried out on the project. This can be rather difficult given the unskilled and manual nature of most projects. Alternatively, training can be arranged that is likely to improve an individual's prospects of getting a permanent job. Now we are getting somewhere, one might think, but no. CP organisers who do wish to provide such vocational training receive no extra money whatsoever to do so, which must act as a marked disincentive to include a training element in a CP project. Even worse, for the unemployed people participating, the costs of any training that is provided are met by a maximum of £10 a week reduction in wages received. The sponsor can also contribute to the costs of training out of his operating fee, but as noted above, he receives no more for providing training.

This lack of vocational training for CP participants was supposed to be changing. In 1984 the Manpower Services Commission (MSC) proposed that up to 50,000 CP places each year should be linked to short courses to basic-skills training and work preparation. Indeed, in the document *Towards an Adult Training Strategy*, the MSC considered that an appropriate option for the future might be to include 13 weeks' skills and work preparation training during the year. Those proposals were dropped from MSC plans because of public expenditure cuts in 1985. But some still find it fairly incredible that within a budget of over £2 billion for 1987–8, the MSC finds it impossible to make the Community Programme anything more than a make-work special measure. As with YTS, the main objective has been to boost the number of places, almost regardless of work content and certainly regardless of training needs.

Other criticisms are concerned with the low rates of pay for CP participants, pay that does not readily reflect the going rate. There may be some disincentive to participate on the part of the unemployed because of this. Compulsion is becoming more common under the 'Restart'-interview procedures, however. There is a pronounced bias in the type of work available. For men, it is typically unskilled manual work. For women participants (now fallen to just one-fifth of those on the scheme) the work most typically involves basic clerical duties. Just one in 20 CP participants now come from the ethnic minorities, a figure that has halved from the first days of the Programme.

While provision on the Community Programme is large, at over 300,000 places during the course of a year, there are over 1.5 million other people who would be eligible. For the vast majority of the long-term unemployed there is nothing at all to cater for their needs: no training or retraining programmes, little in the way of special job subsidies, poor re-employment prospects, and the one large measure designed to help, at whatever low a level and even with its severe shortcomings, takes less than one in five of those who might benefit.

In mid-November 1987, the Secretary of State for Employment announced that in 1988 the Community Programme would be merged with the Job Training Scheme (see below). In all 600,000 places are planned, double the number at present for these two schemes, but at the same cost. The details are patchy at the time of writing (a White Paper has recently appeared) but unemployed participants are expected to continue receiving their unemployment benefit, as under JTS, but with the addition of a small training allowance, possibly of £5 or £10 a week. The new scheme, provisionally entitled 'Training for Life' has already been labelled a 'slave labour scheme' by Opposition spokesmen.

ENTERPRISE ALLOWANCE SCHEME

There has been a large increase in self-employment in the UK in the 1980s (see Chapter 2). Self-employment has been fuelled by the Enterprise Allowance Scheme, which in June 1987 provided financial aid to 90,000 people. According to *Action for Jobs*, 'plenty of unemployed people would like to become self-employed or start their own small business'. They certainly have been doing so in some numbers. About one-third receiving the allowance had been unemployed for a year or longer. Launched nationally in 1983, the scheme provides £40 a week for up to a year for those setting up on their own. This weekly allowance is supposed to partly compensate for the loss of unemployment or supplementary benefit during the early days of a business venture.

To be eligible, people should have been unemployed for at least eight weeks (the time period used to be 13 weeks), and be at least

18-years-old. Access to capital of at least £1000 is required. Obviously a viable business idea is required, but the tests of 'viability' are rather variable. Those in receipt of a scheme allowance are not counted among the unemployed. A whole range of businesses have been set up with help from the Enterprise Allowance Scheme. One enterprising idea which received a great deal of publicity involved two women who became self-employed in Newport with the assistance of the Enterprise Allowance Scheme. They managed to run a brothel for five months before being found out! In court, they pleaded guilty to receiving £1760 from the MSC by deception. There is also some evidence that allowances are going to some of those running unofficial self-employed businesses in the 'hidden economy' while still claiming benefit. The Enterprise Allowance Scheme permits such individuals to become legitimate. It certainly shows some enterprise.

In 1985–6 the Enterprise Allowance Scheme cost over £110 million. It is estimated that about one-half of businesses created with an allowance are still operating some 18 months after starting (that is, six months after entitlement to the allowance has ended).

JOB RELEASE SCHEME

Job Release is the state's official early-retirement scheme. A man or woman can retire one year before normal retirement age (so, aged 64 for men, 59 for women) providing the employer fills the vacancy with somebody officially counted as unemployed. The person retiring up to a year early then receives a weekly allowance until he or she becomes eligible for the state retirement pension. The allowance can be up to £74 per week (married with dependant spouse); it is £52 for a single person.

Job Release in different full-time and part-time forms has been running for a decade. Between 1977 and 1986 over 300,000 people retired early with the aid of the scheme. Once retired in this way, and receiving an allowance, recipients are forbidden to get another job. The employer *has* to agree to the rules on replacement before an employee can retire in this way. The employer retains power of veto. If it goes through, the employer receives a fee to cover administration costs.

In the 1980s early retirement has in any case become much more common, even without the assistance of the Job Release Scheme. Sometimes early retirement is compulsory, sometimes voluntary. It can take place in companies as a way of avoiding redundancy among younger workers, or early retirement may go hand-in-hand with redundancy. Compulsory early retirement is, to all intents and purposes, the redundancy of an older worker. The main objective of such policies within companies has been to reduce their headcount, to save on labour costs. Those retiring early in this way may not be replaced at all, and certainly not with someone who is unemployed. Research from the Institute of Manpower Studies found that 80 per cent of companies who had early-retirement programmes did so in order to reduce their workforces. Such policies at the company level do little, if anything, to diminish the ranks of the unemployed. There are, in addition, proposals from time to time to cut the normal state-retirement age, perhaps to 60 for both men and women. But that is another story (see Chapter 8).

JOBSHARE

Jobshare is puny. In June 1987, there were just 600 new part-time jobs created. Prior to this the statistics showed applications approved, which would have given the figure of about one-half of this. Jobshare is the new name for the Job Splitting Scheme. It too was puny in effect. The idea seemed bright enough. With Job Splitting, an employer who created part-time jobs, or split an existing job in half, and then brought in employees from the dole queue or from a special employment scheme, such as YTS or the Community Programme, then received a grant towards the costs of administration and training. Jobshare aims to create 1000 jobs in its first year (1987–8). Employers now receive £1000 for each part-time job created. Jobshare, like its predecessor, pays an employer if an existing full-time job is divided, or if two new part-time jobs are created, or if part-time jobs result from combining the regular overtime hours of existing full-time workers.

Take-up has been low under both Job Splitting and the new Jobshare. The Job Splitting Scheme resulted in just 1600 jobs being shared in four years. The reasons are not hard to find. Administration can be complicated and certainly costs are higher with two people sharing a single job. Employers argue that the grant available to cover this is too low. It is also argued that only certain jobs actually lend themselves to splitting or sharing in this way. According to early research carried out by the Institute of Manpower Studies, it is estimated that at most 13 per cent of full-time jobs had the potential to be shared. Other problems include a diminution of the employment-protection rights of a full-time employee who then jobshares on a part-time basis. The trade unions dislike jobsharing partly for this reason. From the employers' point of view, it is regarded as a handicap that they *have* to recruit unemployed people to such jobs. From the point of view of the unemployed themselves, or those on special schemes, a shared job is a shared income. In particular, older unemployed men, perhaps with family responsibilities, are unlikely to present themselves for the kinds of jobs that can be shared most easily. And the incomes associated with sharing make it unrealistic even to expect more than a small fraction to be interested.

Jobsharing in some form or another will no doubt stay in the books as a special employment measure. But in anything like its present form it can never be more than a vaguely interesting experiment.

JOBSTART ALLOWANCE

Rather like the New Workers Scheme, the Jobstart Allowance owes its existence to the acceptance of the idea that the unemployed have priced themselves out of work. This is a nice example of the supply-side job subsidy. But unlike the New Workers Scheme (see above) which pays a weekly allowance to the *employer*, Jobstart pays a wages supplement to the *employee*. The Jobstart Allowance was formally announced in the Chancellor of the Exchequer's 1986 Budget, although its existence and many details had been expertly leaked in the preceding months. The scheme started on 1 July 1986, so it is early days yet. In June 1987 7000 people were in receipt of the allowance.

The Jobstart Allowance is specifically aimed at the long-term unemployed: to be eligible you have to be at least 18-years-old and to have been unemployed for at least a year. The scheme provides a £20 a week allowance for six months for unemployed people taking full-time jobs that pay less than £80 a week. When the allowance was announced, Chancellor Nigel Lawson acknowledged that those receiving Jobstart Allowances might well, as a result, be receiving substantially higher pay than those working alongside them in the same jobs with the same employer. They were advised to say nothing about it! The Jobstart scheme is expected to cost £300 million in 1987–8.

Clearly, employment subsidies like Jobstart are part of the supply-sider employment-policy armoury aimed at depressing wages on the labour market. Other weapons, discussed elsewhere in this book, include the abolition of the Wages Councils, the New Workers Scheme subsidy to employers recruiting young people on low wages, poor pay and compulsory attendance on YTS, public-sector pay policy, training on benefit in the Job Training Scheme, cuts in benefits for the unemployed and tighter eligibility, and attempts to drive down reservation wages (i.e. minimum acceptable wages) among the unemployed during their formal interviews on benefit entitlement. This package represents a consistent set of policies.

JOB TRAINING SCHEME

If the Job Training Scheme (JTS) is nothing else, it is controversial. The number of participants on the JTS programme has yet to be included in the monthly table of government employment measures published in the *Employment Gazette*. With its expansion nationally it was intended that JTS should provide 250,000 training places over the course of a year. A network of 350 JTS managing agents were to be providing specialised skills training and practical work experience for the unemployed. It was intended that in all cases JTS should lead to a recognised vocational qualification. The target quarter of a million places were aimed at those aged 18 to 25 who had been unemployed for more than six months. The shorter term target was 110,000 places by the Autumn 1987, although the actual take-up was less than one quarter of this.

Much sabre-rattling took place in the Trades Unions about JTS. Numerous proposals for a boycott were made. The shop-workers union, USDAW, which co-operated fully with the Youth Training Scheme, had grave reservations about the encroachment of JTS into retailing. Garfield Davies, the General Secretary of USDAW, called JTS 'vicious exploitation'. It was feared that while the aim of JTS was purportedly to provide vocational training for the unemployed in order to help them gain employment, the real objective was the promotion of a 'workfare' philosophy and an attempt to drive wages down, with JTS providing another pool of extra-cheap labour.

JTS, in its present form, just provides trainees with their unemployment or supplementary benefit in the form of an allowance whilst in training. Assistance with travel expenses is available, but no additional training allowance of any kind is paid. Norman Willis, TUC General Secretary, has urged the government to provide additional funding through the Manpower Services Commission, 'The rates paid to trainees are dole rates only and are inadequate and unjust'. JTS fitted well into the consistent set of supply side and workfare employment policies being pursued by the Thatcher administration.

JTS is unique among the government's special employment measures. The scheme is a 'work-for-benefits' regime. The pilot programme revealed a drop-out rate as high as a third and a lack of consistency in the training received. It is too early to evaluate its contribution to getting permanent jobs for trainees, but it is likely to have a high substitution effect, with very cheap JTS trainees replacing ordinary workers, or with vacancies going to this group rather than to those who would have to be paid. Recruitment to JTS is carried out through the 'Restart'-interview procedure (see below). Young unemployed claimants who have been out of work long term will have the greatest difficulty in refusing the offer of a

JTS place, if they are not to lose benefit. This element of informal but, none the less real compulsion is likely to undermine even the higher quality training schemes. Compulsory attendance is not altogether healthy for motivation. The training takes between three and 12 months.

In September 1988, JTS is to be combined with the Community Programme and some smaller schemes. The 600,000 participants on this new 'Training for Life' programme will receive just their dole money plus a low level training allowance of between £5 and £10 a week. Unemployed people from the ages of 18 years to retirement age will be eligible. A degree of compulsion is expected. 'We need to have a workforce with tomorrow's skills to compete in tomorrow's world' (Lord Young). Whether the Job Training Scheme and other goverment training initiatives are going to provide this is not in doubt. They will not.

RESTART

'Restart' is less of a special employment measure and more of a set of procedures for assisting the long-term unemployed to come off the unemployment register. Starting in July 1986, all those unemployed for a year or more were 'invited' to attend a Jobcentre for an interview and counselling session. The scale of the inter-viewing has been enormous, with over 1.3 million people in the long-term unemployed category (excluding those already on special schemes like the Community Programme and those unemployed but not eligible for benefit). It was intended that everyone should be interviewed before March 1987, and the inter-views would take place as unemployed people served their one-year sentence. The idea of the interview is to see whether long-term unemployed can be offered a place on the Community Programme, can become self-employed with an Enterprise Allowance, work on a voluntary project or with the JTS or any other training. They might even, perhaps, be offered a job, with or without the assistance of a Jobstart Allowance. At worst, inter-viewees should be offered a place in a Jobclub (see below) or take part in a short Restart course to show them how they might be more effective in job search. In January 1987 it was announced that from the beginning of April Restart interviews would take place with those unemployed for six months. From 10 April to 29 May 1987, 228,852 Restart interviews took place.

Some rather extravagant claims have been made for Restart. In December 1986, for example, the MSC stated that 10 per cent of the 500,000-plus long-term unemployed interviewed by that time had been 'submitted to a job'. This one in ten includes all those who had also been put forward for participation on a special scheme, which is certainly not the same as a job. In the pilot areas for Restart, in fact, just 1 per cent of those interviewed got a job: a further 3 per cent obtained a place on the Community Programme. The MSC now claims that up to 15 per cent of those interviewed have gone on to the Community Programme, but in the pilots four times more people were offered a CP placement than actually got one.

The invitation to attend for a Restart interview makes it very clear that attendance is not voluntary. A failure to attend can (and often does) result in the loss of benefit. Critics of Restart suggest that the procedure has more to do with frightening the unemployed out of claiming benefits or scaring off those claiming benefit and earning, than really assisting the unemployed. Certainly, in the early days up to one in ten 'invited' to come for a Restart interview failed to do so.

What Restart does, if nothing else, is to draw the attention of the unemployed to the different special employment and training measures available. And for every person placed this is one person fewer in the monthly unemployment count, however temporary this might be. Once time has been spent on a measure like the Community Programme and, if the individual concerned then becomes unemployed again, then he or she is no longer long-term unemployed, officially. Lord Young himself, speaking over Christmas 1986, had to agree that Restart, where it did find work for the long-term unemployed, involved a redistribution of jobs in favour of the unemployed. One can justify this on social grounds, but it is important to emphasise that Restart will not create a single new job on its own. The job subsidies towards which Restart interviewees might be directed, will of course have some net job-creation effect.

During 1987 additional resources have also been put into Job-clubs. The 200 Jobclubs in existence in the autumn of 1986 were expanded to 1000 by March 1987. 'Jobclubs aim to help long-term unemployed people help themselves in their search for work' (*Action for Jobs*). Jobclubs are run by Jobcentre employees, and aim to 'restore self-confidence and improve job-hunting techniques'. The unemployed are expected to follow up at least ten jobs a day, apparently. Of more practical help, the Jobclub provides facilities such as telephones, stationery, newspapers, photocopying and typewriters to help in chasing up and applying for jobs. But of course, if there are no jobs available, even the very best facilities and counselling assistance will be to no avail.

OTHER MEASURES

The main special employment and training measures have been discussed above. There are others. Four main types of scheme are available—employment, training, enterprise and special needs. The *Action for Jobs* booklet lists 26 separate schemes or projects for the unemployed under those four headings. Some of the other projects are concerned with the unemployed doing voluntary work, but retaining their rights to unemployment or supplementary benefit. The Voluntary Projects Programme is the biggest, with over 300 projects running nationwide. Somewhat curiously, this scheme is listed under the 'Employment' heading in *Action for Jobs*. Some schemes provide support to employers in their training programmes; another gives loans to individuals so that they may pay for vocational training. There is some assistance for special disadvantaged groups, in particular the disabled, including a short-term jobs subsidy. The full summary listing can be scrutinised in *Action for Jobs*, available to anyone from Jobcentres. Being unemployed yourself is not a requirement to acquire the booklet. Supplementary leaflets give full details of each of the schemes.

CONCLUSIONS

At the 1986 Conservative Party Conference, Lord Young, then Secretary of State for Employment, offered this message to the unemployed: 'You have not been forgotten, you will not be forgotten, for that you have my word'. Lord Young is now at the Department of Trade and Industry. In keeping the jobless in his government's collective memory, Lord Young was particularly thinking of the range of special measures introduced or greatly expanded since 1979. In the summer of 1987 there were over 700,000 people taken out of the unemployment count as a result of these measures. And this did not include programmes like the Job Training Scheme.

On the training front, the Youth Training scheme is confused in its objectives—at one and the same time it is attempting to be a rapid unemployment-alleviation measure for young people, and also to provide quality training. Since its inauguration, the temporary unemployment-alleviation dimension has outweighed the quality-training dimension. In 1988 up to 100,000 16- and 17-year-olds will lose entitlement to supplementary benefit if they refuse a place on YTS: between 20,000 and 30,000 young people who refused to go onto YTS, plus a further 70,000 leaving the scheme part-way through. There are 480,000 two-year YTS places available. A quality vocational-training programme with a proper forward-looking labour-market perspective that leads to jobs should not need compulsion. For the older unemployed person, increasing emphasis is being given to JTS, essentially training and work on benefit. This is the closest yet to workfare initiatives that we have seen this side of the Atlantic. Cheap labour for the employer, a patchy quality of training and no financial incentive inevitably leads to motivation problems.

The National Audit Office, in a 1987 report to Parliament, severely castigated the Department of Employment and the MSC for spending over £1 billion a year on training schemes without having any real idea of the current and future skill needs of industry. Without such an important labour-market perspective, of course, training programmes are also perpetrating a fraud on unemployed participants. If training does lead to a job then it is rather more by good fortune than design.

Job subsidies are used to aid the hiring of unemployed young workers (New Worker Scheme) and the older long-term unemployed (Jobstart Allowance). In the former the subsidy is paid to the employer, in the latter it goes to the employee accepting a low-paid job. Job subsidies of this kind do have a large element of deadweight and substitution effect in their make-up. This serves to substantially increase the cost of each new job created. Job subsidies of a kind certainly do have a place in the reduction of unemployment, but they do need to be carefully fine-tuned to maximise the new job-creation effects. Attaching a credit to individuals in special locations or with special disadvantages might help more (see Chapter 9).

The Community Programme is at present the largest measure for the older unemployed worker. It is a make-work programme, with individuals working on projects that carry out socially useful tasks that would not otherwise be undertaken. The pay is low, there is little, if any, training, and CP is designed to discourage training. Participants are not equipped with vocational skills that may assist them to obtain permanent jobs. The number of places available for the long-term unemployed on CP and other schemes, falls far short of the numbers eligible. Restart cannot offer all those unemployed for six months or longer anything of substance. A desk, a newspaper and a kind word is all that many Jobclub 'members' can hope for.

The UK, like many other countries (see Chapter 6), has seen the unemployment industry grow like Topsy in the 1980s. Special employment and training measures abound, all with deficiencies and problems. The one employment measure that has been carefully steered away from in the UK is direct intervention in the form of public-sector job-creation. Indeed, under the Thatcher administration since 1979, public-sector job-*destruction* has been the order of the day. Instead, what has been pursued, at times with manic enthusiasm, is a consistent set of supply-side interventions on the labour market. These have taken the form (see Chapter 3) of benefit cuts and lower reservation wages for the unemployed, attempting to increase the quality of labour, reducing the number of people officially available for work, increasing the income differential between the employed and unemployed, reducing employment protection and giving more power to employers. The special employment and training measures discussed above fit very neatly into this view of what has caused unemployment and what the appropriate supply-side responses might be.

There is another view of what has caused high unemployment, which many economists and others would agree is more convincing and stands a closer scrutiny (see Chapter 3). The acceptance of evidence from the demand-siders on this, unavoidably leads to the conclusion that the Thatcher government's measures cannot work. Job subsidies and training and socially useful schemes can make a contribution, and who would bet that they will not still exist ten years from now in some form or another. But they cannot cure the crisis of unemployment. They tackle symptoms, not causes, and it is remedial action on causes that is long overdue.

Mrs Thatcher is wrong; there is an alternative.

8. The Choices for Unemployment

One may be forgiven for thinking, from what we have seen so far in this book, that the government and the supply-siders have had something of a monopoly in proposing ways on alleviating unemployment, mainly through altering the mechanisms of the labour market. In particular, action has been taken on reducing wages and the wages expectations of the unemployed, increasing the quality of unemployed labour through various training schemes; labour supply is being reduced, work has been redistributed, benefits have been cut and the power of organised labour has been deliberately eroded.

It has been argued throughout that these measures have been adopted partly for ideological reasons, partly because of an urge to get the market for labour operating in a way analogous to the market for apples, and most importantly, because of a flawed understanding of just what has caused the present crisis of unemployment. It is the Conservative government's economic policy itself that bears the heaviest responsibility for the current predicament of 4 million unemployed.

There has, in fact, been no shortage of alternative proposals to reduce unemployment, some even emanating from within the ranks of the Conservative Party itself, from the so-called 'wets'. At the time of both the 1986 and 1987 Budgets, dissident groups were calling for the postponement of income tax cuts because of their low impact on job-creation, in comparison with targeted public-spending measures. The arguments went unheeded. Indeed, all non-supply-side ideas aimed at reducing unemployment have fallen on deaf ears. The government has not been at all receptive to any proposed policy measures to substantially cut unemployment, however well worked out and whatever the likely degree of success. This chapter will consider a number of these alternative strategies and their rationale, and Chapter 9 sets out a radical programme to cut unemployment to a million or fewer in the years to 1995.

The calling of a General Election for June 1987 required the other political parties to focus their attention on their own policies to cut unemployment. They needed to marshall their thoughts in a coherent way and set out their programmes before the electorate. It was thought that, if the electorate could be convinced of these policies for unemployment, it would make a major contribution to determining the election result. Unfortunately (for the unemployed at least), people rarely vote on single issues: when voting the electorate has to 'buy' a bundle of policies and personalities, some of which are going to be more attractive for some than for others. Any claims of a mandate for a single policy in an election manifesto are bogus. While the pollsters still maintained that unemployment was indeed a key issue, defence, the trade unions, privatisation and shares, and a host of other social, economic and political issues were also of significance. The rest is history.

THE LABOUR PARTY PROGRAMME

The first element in the Labour Party's 1987 General Election Manifesto 'priority programme' was the Jobs Programme. With the election being called not long after the publication of the party's *New Jobs for Britain*, both the background and more detailed work of cutting unemployment had already been carried out. The manifesto committed an incoming Labour government to cut unemployment by one million:

> We will reduce unemployment by one million in two years as the first instalment of beating mass unemployment.
> Half a million jobs will be generated in private industry and in the public sector by the repairing and building of the houses, hospitals and schools, the transport improvements and sewers that the nation needs. This will be achieved by public investment and by reducing employers' National Insurance contributions in targeted areas.
> Another 360,000 new jobs and training places will be created. This will provide new skills for young people and adults — with proper opportunities for women.

A further 300,000 new jobs will improve the health and education services and the neglected community and caring services. We will extend the voluntary Job Release Scheme to men over 60 so that those who want to retire early vacate jobs for those who are currently unemployed. This could take as many as 160,000 people out of unemployment and into work.

It was estimated by the Labour Party that their jobs and anti-poverty programmes would cost some £6 billion a year for the two years to mid-1989. The 1987 Budget income tax cut from 29p in the £ to 27p was to be reversed, raising just over £2 billion. Increased government borrowing by £3 billion would make up most of the difference. Increased taxation on the richest 5 per cent of the population would raise a bit extra, although it is arguable whether this would have been imposed for revenue-raising or redistribution reasons.

These proposals were far more limited than those for a more radical economic strategy coming from parts of the Labour Party in the earlier 1980s. This strategy included such elements as:

- expansion in aggregate demand, through public-spending increases, tax cuts for below-average earners, tax increases for high-income groups;
- increased government borrowing;
- price controls (for a limited period);
- import controls;
- exchange controls;
- redistribution of income and wealth through taxation;
- nationalisation of major companies, planning agreements with the rest;
- withdrawal from the European Economic Community.

Certainly, the policy ideas to reduce unemployment contained in the 1987 Labour Party manifesto were comparatively conservative. There was to be no massive and indiscriminate expansion of the economy, no huge increase in taxation or government borrowing to pay for a back-to-work programme. The medium-term ambitions were modest—and achievable, with some caveats. Table 8.1 reveals the details of Labour's calculations. The annual net outlay came in at just under £6 billion, as noted above. Almost half the jobs to be created were expected to be in the private sector, with two-fifths of these being in manufacturing industry. In comparison with earlier proposals, the role of the local authorities and nationalised industries in creating new jobs was much more muted, although they were still expected to make a contribution.

In the field of training (a supply-side measure) Labour were proposing 75,000 traineeships for the adult unemployed, although

Table 8.1: Labour Party job-creation proposals, 1987

Activity	Jobs or places	Number off unemployment register	Average net annual cost (£ million) over 2 years
Economic enterprise[a]	250,000	200,000	1,000
Capital investment in infrastructure	250,000	180,000	1,900
Raising quality of services	300,000	220,000	2,000
Training for skills	360,000	355,000	800
Job Release Scheme	–	160,000	200
Total	1,160,000	1,115,000	5,900

Note: a. Including cuts in employers' national insurance contributions.

definitely not in the mould of the Job Training Scheme. There were to be 100,000 training places based on project-work to replace part of the Community Programme; and 75,000 traineeships would have been created for young people, with a further 75,000 places for other young people remaining unemployed after participating on YTS or after leaving further education. An educational maintenance allowance to encourage young people from poorer families to stay on at school, and the recruitment of 30,000 trainers were also part of the package. In all, the training measures alone were expected to lead to 360,000 people being taken off the unemployment register.

The capital-investment programme would have created jobs in the construction industry and areas of high unemployment. Labour-intensive repair work was to be the particular target. According to the Conservative government's figures, over £23-billion work of repair work are needed urgently in local authority housing, schools and in other public buildings. The Association of Metropolitan Authorities estimate that a further £27-billion worth of work is now required on the nation's private-housing stock to bring it up to scratch. Who can deny the common sense of bringing the jobs that urgently need to be done together with those who need jobs?

Under the heading of raising the quality of services (see Table 8.1) Labour proposed funding 65,000 more home-helps to meet the growing needs of the elderly and 14,000 more nursery school teachers, perhaps the single most neglected area in UK education. Left rather vaguer in terms of relative size, employment expansion was also proposed in the National Health Service, non-nursery teaching jobs, the factory inspectorate, tax staff, customs officials, the Post Office, British Rail and clerical staff for the Department of Health and Social Security. Over 200,000 jobs in total were to be funded under these different headings.

Naturally enough, in 1987 the power-wielding Conservative government poured scorn on the Labour proposals for new jobs, with the then Secretary of State for Employment, Lord Young, arguing that the Labour proposals as a whole would lead to a million more people being made unemployed. Kenneth Clarke called the proposals 'incredible' and 'not worked out'. This was clearly political gamesmanship for electoral purposes, and neither comment had any basis in fact. Indeed, an analysis of Conservative, Labour and SDP–Liberal Alliance policies from the Oxford Economic Forecasting Group in 1987 demonstrated just how effective at unemployment alleviation such a mix of demand- and supply-based changes could be.

Of course, various assumptions had to be built into the Oxford Economic Forecasting Group's projections. Assuming Conservative policy stayed on track with further tax cuts, small public-spending increases, further privatisation, a tight grip on government borrowing and a stable value of sterling, registered unemployment was forecast to stay at about the 3 million level throughout the period from 1987 to 1991. Balance of payments deficits, especially severe in 1989, and inflation creeping up to 5 per cent again also characterised the Tory forecast. For our purposes, the most important thing is no substantial change in unemployment.

For the Labour Party, public-spending growth and some tax increases were assumed. Inflation rising to 6.2 per cent before dropping back to 5 per cent was part of the price to be paid for unemployment being cut to 2.3 million by 1991. However, two other key elements that had to be included in order to achieve this level of unemployment cut were a 10 per cent devaluation of sterling (i.e. making exports cheaper and imports dearer) and, more problematically, some kind of incomes policy or agreement that would restrict earnings growth to a maximum 8 per cent a year. But maybe a shaving up on inflation, together with action on sterling and incomes, would be a small price to pay to have 'only' 2.3 million unemployed?

In fact, at the 1987 election and in its jobs programme, the Labour Party set its face firmly against any kind of incomes policy. This was in sharp contrast to the policy platform of the Alliance (see below). In reviewing the Labour jobs programme, outsiders did express concern about the possible effects on the balance of payments, interest rates and wage inflation. However, by firmly rejecting calls from within the party for a general untargeted expansion of the economy, which would most likely increase imports and lead to extra spending being diverted into wage increases rather than job-creation, a carefully considered route was chosen that would minimise these likely problems. Training, public-employment expansion, particularly in the lower-paid jobs most suitable for the unemployed, and infrastructure investment were least likely to have adverse knock-on economic effects, particularly when on the relatively modest scale proposed.

Each extra person taken out of the dole queue saves the Exchequer £6000 a year in terms of benefit saved and additional tax revenue gained. Unemployment is now costing the country over £20 billion a year. On economic grounds, then, as well as on social and personal, some the elements of the Labour Party's jobs programme have to be carefully considered. But maybe what used to be the SDP–Liberal Alliance also had something to offer. It will be interesting to see in future years just how the two reconstituted parties diverge on unemployment-alleviation measures, as well as on other issues.

THE SDP–LIBERAL ALLIANCE (1987)

In the 1987 General Election campaign, the Alliance committed themselves to reduce unemployment by one million within three years. This would require the creation of half a million jobs a year—1.5 million jobs in all (see below). The Alliance too had the relief of unemployment well to the fore in its programme of economic and social policies. As the manifesto set out clearly:

> Worst of all is unemployment. Many more than the three million people registered as unemployed have no jobs. The Government has juggled the figures and brought in cosmetic devices to hide the truth. But the facts won't go away. The dole queue is three times what it was in 1979. Unemployment has been a low priority for this government, used to keep down inflation. Tax cuts have had a higher priority than job creation. The cost in human misery and hardship, loss of confidence and self-respect, not least among young people, has been incalculable.

In terms of target unemployed groups, the priority of the Alliance was the alleviation of unemployment among the long-term unemployed (i.e. those unemployed for a year or more) and amongst young people. A special feature of the Alliance programme for jobs was the provision of a job guarantee for the long-term unemployed. This was to be done through:

(a) a building and investment programme aimed at providing

200,000 jobs in such essential areas as transport, housing, insulation, urban renewal and new technologies;

(b) a new recruitment incentive to encourage companies to take on over 270,000 jobless people;

(c) a crash programme of education and training, offering new skills to the unskilled unemployed, with 200,000 places;

(d) 60,000 extra jobs in the health and social services to improve care in the community and more jobs in nursery education;

(e) an expanding job release scheme, opening up 30,000 jobs by allowing men to benefit from the scheme at 62 years of age.

A cut of one-quarter in the employers' national insurance contributions in areas of high unemployment was expected to encourage employers to recruit more staff (an earlier document suggested that the Alliance should cut the contribution by 20 per cent, creating 80,000 more jobs). Increased public spending was supposed to have been targeted on those areas that would 'increase output and exports rather than consumption and imports'. Capital investment would build up to £1.5 billion a year, to be spent on transport, housing, schools, hospitals and drainage. The joy of such increased public spending is that it does tend to be spent in the UK, on home-produced materials, goods and services. Tax cuts, unless they really do focus on the least well-off, will be largely spent on imports. This creates jobs abroad rather than at home, and is bad for the balance of payments (i.e. the difference between how much we export, and how much is imported). The recruitment incentive to employers referred to above (see (b) in the Alliance shopping list) was expected to be a jobs subsidy of £2000 for one year to employers recruiting the long-term unemployed.

So, it can be seen that the Alliance policies to cut unemployment were, once again, a combination of demand- and supply-side measures. It is the Conservatives who stand alone of the political parties in failing to appreciate that failings on the demand side of the economy need correcting in order to reduce unemployment. Income tax cuts do stimulate demand, do stimulate consumer spending, it is true, but the Tories' main reasons for engaging in such cuts relate to debates about taxation and incentives, and not about job-creation. And even if income tax cuts do result in increases in demand, it is very much an expensive 'mud-thrown-at-non-stick-wall' approach. Some of the extra spending may create some jobs for some of the unemployed. Most will not.

The extra revenue to fund the anti-unemployment policies of the Alliance were expected to come from an increase in government borrowing of £4 billion. Extra, windfall tax receipts coming from the consumer spending and company-profits boom, additional income tax receipts and economic growth, at present earmarked by the Conservatives for further cuts in taxation and government borrowing, would also be used for spending on job-creation and training. Further privatisation proceeds would also have been used in this way. The maths does add up. There were two other elements in the Alliance programme of particular note: an incomes policy and action on the value of sterling. Where the Labour Party had little of any substance to say on incomes policy, and the Conservatives use a mixture of high unemployment, benefits changes, tax cuts, public-sector pay policy and exhortation to try and limit the growth of earnings, the Alliance were putting forward what their spokesman Ian Wrigglesworth called a 'carrot and stick' approach to an incomes strategy. The Alliance idea was for a counter-inflation tax, whereby firms with over one hundred employees who deviated from a nationally agreed pay-increase norm would find themselves the target of a special new tax, effectively bumping up labour costs even more. It was thought that this would provide a sufficient disincentive to employers to concede high pay rises. It was to be a long-term measure, the argument against previous incomes policies being that they were crude in application, were temporary and when abandoned after relatively short periods, led to large pay increases. The counter-inflation tax was criticised for penalising successful organisations and their employees, and may even have fuelled inflation when the wage increase and special tax were passed on in the form of higher prices to the consumer. Profit-sharing and share-option schemes were expected to make the tax acceptable for high-flying organisations: in fact, such concessions would have been likely to form the escape valve for the incomes policy. The counter-inflation tax would have been a nightmare to administer. In spite of Alliance estimates that a cap on earnings growth through the imposition of the new tax would have helped to create an additional 300,000 jobs, there is widespread disbelief at this. This form of incomes policy was simply a gimmick.

Perhaps more usefully the Alliance proposed that the UK and sterling joined the European Monetary System (EMS). We may well still do this in any case. The EMS is a kind of currency club which aims to keep the relative values of the different currencies (e.g. franc, lira, mark) within clearly defined boundaries, with assistance given to any single currency that for one reason or another may be subject to temporary pressures, either upwards or downwards. Joining the EMS, sometimes called the monetary snake, at a competitive rate, was expected to lead to a 2 per cent drop in UK interest rates. Were this to be the effect then some 150,000 jobs could be created. Certainly, a 1 per cent cut in interest rates leads to more than three times as many jobs being created as a 1 per cent cut in income tax. There are grave doubts, however, that simply joining the EMS would produce the interest-rate cut expected. Increased government borrowing in fact tends to put a little upward pressure on interest rates.

So, the Alliance also set out policies for incomes and the rate of exchange. The job-creation effects anticipated were, however, frankly unbelievable. The gimmicky counter-inflation tax was likely to have unlooked-for side-effects and was unwieldy. There were doubts whether the Alliance policies for sterling could deliver on interest rates. The policies, taken in combination, would have cut unemployment. The Oxford Economic Forecasting Group estimated that with government spending rising by 3 per cent year, membership of the EMS and an incomes policy that could deliver a maximum 5 per cent incomes growth, unemployment would fall to 2.6 million by 1991. Inflation would have been steady at 3.5 to 4 per cent a year in the period to 1991. Balance-of-payments experiences would be similar to those of the Conservative and Labour Parties.

From their 1987 programmes, then, both Labour and Alliance parties would have made some inroads into the problem of unemployment. Neither inflation nor the balance of payments would have been a disaster had the Conservative Party lost the 1987 General Election. They did not lose, and under existing policies the future represents little change for the unemployed. Other organisations and individuals have also set out their own policies for jobs. Some have been influential in shaping the proposed policies of the Opposition parties.

TRADE UNIONS

Naturally enough, many of the ideas of the Labour Party for cutting unemployment had as their source the trade unions. The annual March Budget is the time when many union research departments dust down their calculators and put forward proposals on what the Chancellor should and should not contemplate in his forthcoming speech. In the years since 1979 public spending and taxation changes organised in order to reduce unemployment have tended to dominate the trade unions' messages to the Chancellor. On all occasions, he has studiously ignored such pleas, often rubbishing the policies and their objectives in the process.

For 1987, the Trade Union Congress (TUC) put forward proposals that aimed to create 600,000 jobs in the first year and 800,000 jobs over two years. The total cost was estimated at £6.5 billion, including an additional £2.4 billion to be spent on public investment in construction, repair and maintenance. Out of the job-gain total of 800,000 it was forecast that 550,000 of these jobs would go to people currently on the official unemployment register. Manufacturing industry was expected to gain, in all, some 250,000 jobs. The TUC were assisted by the National Institute of Economic and Social Research and the London Business School in preparing estimates of the employment effects of their expansionary budget.

Many individual trade unions have also prepared job pro-grammes. There is insufficient space here (and little point) in going through them all in detail. They do often represent a kind of special pleading on behalf of their own members. One of more than passing interest, however, is that prepared by the National Union of Public Employees (NUPE) in 1987. As public-sector job-creation is frequently put forward as potentially a major contributor to unemployment alleviation, the role of local authorities, other public-service employers and the nationalised industries in this, together with the attitudes of their respective unions, is of clear importance. The mathematics of NUPE work out slightly differently from that of the TUC. In common with the Labour Party and the TUC, NUPE are looking for growth in the public services as a key to reducing unemployment. NUPE make the point, quite correctly, that new public-service jobs in the main come cheap. An employ-ment growth of 8 per cent in the public services over a two-year period has a cost-per-job of £9400. The proposal for 400,000 new jobs in the public services would cost, then, some £3.8 billion. In addition to work in the public sector, it was estimated that 200,000 new jobs in the private sector of industry and commerce would be created as a result of the knock-on effects of increasing public spending. NUPE spelt out in some detail just where these new public-service jobs might be targeted. They included 100,000 in the National Health Service, including 46,000 nurses, 8000 doctors, and 22,000 ancillary workers. Employment in education would rise by 120,000, including 50,000 teachers and lecturers and 34,000 manual workers. In the social services 30,000 more staff would be taken on. Unskilled and semi-skilled jobs would also be available in refuse collection (6000) and in parks and recreation (8000). While some of these jobs clearly would meet the needs of the unemployed, doctors and lecturers are not especially numerous among the ranks of the jobless! The training and employment of additional doctors, for example, would, of course, eventually lead to the necessary recruitment of less-skilled health workers. But the time lag is long and such job-creation needs to be related closely to places in education and training, the existence of suitable qualified candi-dates for places in higher and further education, additional training capacity and the existence of trainers themselves. A thoroughgoing education and manpower plan for public-service employment for the mid-1990s could take account of these factors. Just to say that 8000 doctors and 50,000 additional lecturers and teachers can and will be recruited is not particularly helpful. However, the point is usefully made that a similar amount of money can buy you at least twice as many jobs in the public services as in infrastructure investment, and five times as many jobs as income tax cuts. More of this below.

CONSERVATIVE DISSIDENTS

Following the third General Election victory for Mrs Thatcher, this group were less numerous and certainly less vocal than they were in the earlier 1980s. Mr Edward Heath, the former Prime Minister, continues to be associated with the Employment Institute and the Charter for Jobs campaign. He still voices grave misgivings about government policy and unemployment, but his statements go unheeded by the decision-takers in the Conservative Party. Peter Walker's view that unemployment would be a major vote-loser for the government (October 1985) was not borne out by the events of June 1987. Mr Walker considered that 'unemployment is now potentially as big a vote-loser in the tree-lined suburbs as it is in the decaying inner cities'. He was wrong.

The Tory Reform Group, at the time of the 1987 Budget, urged the Chancellor to spend more on urban renewal and housing rather than engage in income tax cuts. The Tory Reform Group, home to the non-monetarist liberals and Tory 'wets', set out a programme for change that had more in common with many non-Conservative politicians. The Group were looking for cuts in employer and employee national insurance contributions and benefit increases for the long-term unemployed. Among other policy changes the Tory Reform Group wanted extra spending in urban areas, tax incentives for private investment in infrastructure and increased capital allowances for building and works. Peter Walker is President of the Group; other patrons included Douglas Hurd, Kenneth Baker, Kenneth Clarke and Viscount Whitelaw. Ministerial positions clearly dampen down (or rather dry out) some Conservative politicians' enthusiasm for such anti-Thatcherite proposals.

CHARTER FOR JOBS

The Charter for Jobs was launched in 1985 as the campaigning wing of the Employment Institute. The Charter is backed by many of the great and the good from UK politics, economics, industry and commerce and trade unions, including Edward Heath, Lord Callaghan, Lord Wilson, Shirley Williams, Lord Ezra and Sir Richard O'Brien. Professor Richard Layard, from the London School of Economics, and his associates provide much of the academic muscle for the Charter and the Institute. The work of the group has already been quoted elsewhere in this book. They are a level-headed, all-party group whose policies for unemployment have much to commend them.

The Charter for Jobs, after reviewing the evidence, concludes that the rise in unemployment in the UK since the late 1970s

mainly reflects low demand. They urge the immediate implementation of three main policy measures:

- a job guarantee for the 1.3 million long-term unemployed;
- a substantial increase in public spending on infrastructure
  investment, with a particular focus on labour-intensive projects;
- a cut in the 'tax on labour', the employers' national insurance
  contributions.

Charter for Jobs have identified £93-billion worth of infrastructure
work that requires urgent attention, including work on housing,
schools, hospitals, water and sewerage mains, and on roads. This
work alone could keep a million people employed for six years.
The first document from Charter for Jobs *We Can Cut Unemployment*,
provides details of their policies, reasons for implementation and
effects. It debunks the notion that such policies need be inflation-
ary. The government has, so often repeated, parrot-fashion, that
any alternative job-creating programmes would lead to hyper-
inflation reappearing, phoenix-like, from the ashes of Thatcherism,
that it is now widely believed. No doubt, economists and Opposition party politicians bear a heavy responsibility here for not
explaining in an accessible way why this would not be the case.
This is clearly a task for the future, although 'Understanding
Economic Policy' is not included among Education Minister
Kenneth Baker's topics for the national core curriculum in the
schools. As Charter for Jobs, and many others, have pointed out,
the government's economic stance in the 1980s has been highly
deflationary, causing unemployment. With so much slack in the
economy, and with expansionary measures targeted on the
unemployed, there is no good reason in economics for thinking
that inflation would let rip. The Charter for Jobs have this
absolutely correct.

RICHARD LAYARD AND FRIENDS

Professor Layard and his associates have been very influential in
shaping the unemployment policies of the SDP–Liberal Alliance
and Charter for Jobs. Consistently throughout the 1980s Richard
Layard, often with Stephen Nickell, has set out a closely argued
line on the causes of unemployment and its remedies. They reject
the Thatcherite and supply-sider interpretations of causes and
have urged a shift in policy towards the expansion of the economy.
However, in common with other more thoughtful critics of the
supply-siders, they argue that in bringing unemployment down
towards the million mark we have to reject the notion of a general
economic expansion. Rather, a combination of targeted demand-

side measures, and further activity on the supply of labour (e.g. training and subsidies) can make substantial inroads into unemployment. Layard and Nickell have also been putting forward the case for an incomes policy through the counter-inflation tax (see section above on SDP–Liberal Alliance). There are a number of important elements in the Layard package, discussed in his book *How to Beat Unemployment* that need to be attended to. Layard sets out five main features of his jobs programme:

1. Additional demand must be targeted at high-unemployment groups; in particular, the long-term unemployed, semi- and unskilled workers, high-unemployment regions, construction workers and young people.
2. The net cost per new job created should be as low as possible.
3. The supply of labour should be improved.
4. The private sector should be promoted in preference to the public sector, where possible.
5. A firm incomes policy has to be introduced.

There are the guiding principles of the Layard package. The main elements for unemployment alleviation would be:

1. A new deal for the long-term unemployed.
2. Restructuring employers' national insurance contributions in favour of the unskilled and the regions.
3. More investment on the infrastructure, involving the construction industry.
4. A new incentive to employers to train their workers.
5. A tax-based incomes policy.

In terms of specific policies for the unemployed, Layard, naturally enough, adopts a multi-pronged stance. The guarantee of a job lasting at least one year for the long-term unemployed person is a main element of the Layard programme. Work on the maintenance, repair and construction of houses, schools, hospitals and roads is proposed. New jobs in community and health care for the long-term unemployed should be created. Private employers would be paid £40 a week for a year if they recruit from the ranks of the long-term unemployed. Layard also proposes an increase in welfare-benefit levels for the working poor, acting as an incentive for the unemployed to take advantage of the job guarantee. When up and running properly, benefit would be refused to those not taking part in the work programme.

Layard aims to try to price the unskilled unemployed into jobs by restructuring employers' national insurance contributions, the so-called tax on jobs. Layard suggests that an 8 per cent cut in the overall costs of employing a less skilled worker could increase the demand for such labour by as much as 16 per cent. The proposal is that no employer's contribution should be levied on workers whose earnings fall below £90 per week (1985). A proportional national insurance of 24 per cent thereafter would raise a similar revenue to the Exchequer as the current contribution scale. Increases in employment in the high-unemployment 'assisted' regions of the country could be rewarded by an exemption from employers' national insurance contributions.

Increased spending on infrastructure investment is also proposed, using unemployed construction workers and the less skilled. Jobs created through house building and road improvements would mainly lie in the private sector. Layard also makes suggestions for improving education and training and for making the housing market more flexible to permit labour mobility.

It can be seen that Richard Layard and friends, along with most of the organisations dealt with so far in this chapter, envisage a marrying of demand and supply side initiatives in order to cut unemployment. This is the only course that can work for the UK in the 1990s.

ODDS AND SODS

Naturally, there has to be an element of selectivity in the choice of unemployment-alleviation measures discussed in this chapter. Proposals have been extremely numerous during the high-unemployment years. The title of this section does not aim to be disparaging about some of the remedies considered here, but it does aim to present the reader with a spectrum of some of the other ideas being put forward.

The Policy Analysis Unit of the National Council for Voluntary Organisations (NCVO) in 1985 set out in a discussion document some of their ideas for the relief of long-term unemployment (*The Long Term Unemployed: Action for a Forgotten Million*). In a somewhat gloomy prognosis, the NCVO considered high long-term unemployment to be a continuing feature of the 1990s, in spite of the possible adoption of policies to expand the economy, a growth in special schemes and job subsidies. The discussion paper called for the setting up of a committee of inquiry to examine the options for the relief of long-term unemployment. It argued the case for the start of a two-tier universal programme for the long-term unemployed. One tier, to last a year, would be an uprated Community Programme, involving training, preparation for work and the rate for the job. The second tier would be a Personal Development Programme, without time limit, with a credit top-up to benefit for participants. One million new places were proposed for this second tier, which might involve volunteer work or training of some kind but not temporary employment.

Professor Paul Cook of Brunel University has been seeking a commitment from employers to pledge an additional job for every £1 million of profits made. With company profits so buoyant a semblance of social (and local) responsibility on the part of more employing organisations certainly could create some jobs. Apparently, the builders John Laing (profits £30 million), have pledged 30 new jobs as a result of Paul Cook's work. But it seems that many of the biggest profit-makers have been studiously ignoring pleas for job-creation.

Members of the British Institute of Management (BIM) urged the Chancellor to increase public spending in each of the five years to 1987. For the 1987 Budget three-quarters of BIM managers would rather have seen public expenditure rise rather receive tax cuts. In particular, extra infrastructure spending was looked for, especially in the growing backlog of repairs and renewals in schools, hospitals, roads and in the sewer system. Investment in science and technology, and an easing of the unemployment and poverty traps were also called for.

Other ideas include the conversion of all overtime into full-time jobs: one-third of all operatives in manufacturing do overtime, on average over eight hours each week. There may be some potential here for unemployment alleviation on the basis of agreement between individual employers and their employees, or in particular industrial sectors. The reduction of the working week to 35 hours would certainly produce jobs. According to work published in the *Employment Gazette*, unemployment could fall by 350,000 with a shorter working week, but at the expense of increasing labour costs by over 8 per cent. Bringing down the male retirement age to 60 years, the same as for women, is also often canvassed: such a change would cost £1.5 billion in increases to the social security bill for pensions, without any guarantee that vacancies created would go to the unemployed. An extension of the government Job Release Scheme might make more sense.

A report from the right-wing Institute of Economic Affairs in May 1987 suggested that the dole queue could be cut by 500,000 if restrictions on rent levels were abolished. *The Housing Morass* outlines a programme to cut benefits and raise council and private rents to market levels over a five-year period. The authors (who included Patrick Minford) argued that unemployed people in council housing should pay the higher rents with no increase in state benefits. This would increase the incentive to work, and the incentive to move in search of work, if necessary. As noted elsewhere in this book, Minford has also been proposing that the unemployed should receive a maximum welfare benefit of 70 per cent of previous after-tax income. Minford remains unconcerned about the effects of differential house prices for the owner-occupier in different regions. In his book, *Unemployment: Cause and Cure,*

Minford is quite happy to state that: 'The house market does not obstruct mobility'.

This is clearly nonsense. Minford's other proposals for unemployment include the further downgrading of trade union influence, wage cuts for the low paid, erosion of employment protection and health and safety regulations, the introduction of 'workfare' and the tightening up of eligibility rules for benefit. All this is on top of 'benefit-capping' and the introduction of higher, market-level rents. In fact, a 10 per cent cut in benefits would lead to a drop of only 150,000 in unemployment, but this is all good supply-side and free-market stuff. Minford also goes along with the government's ideas on income tax cuts.

INCOME TAX CUTS AND PUBLIC EXPENDITURE

The 1980s years of high unemployment have been characterised by lively debates between economists and between politicians (even those within the Conservative Party) on the proper course to steer over taxation, public spending and government borrowing. Since 1979 the government have been committed to lower rates of income tax and to reining-back public spending. These policies derive from a firm belief in the disincentive effects of prevailing levels of income tax in the UK particularly, it seems, for the higher paid, and concerns about the role of the state in economic and social affairs. On taxation, while the income tax rates may have fallen, the overall burden of taxation has increased since 1979: this has had a deflationary effect. Cuts in public spending have also resulted in higher unemployment, with the costs of unemployment itself then feeding back through to public spending on transfer payments to support the unemployed.

We do now know rather a lot about the potential for job-creation and the relative costs of tax cuts, special employment measures and public-spending increases. If the government borrows an extra £1 billion, and then uses this money to cut income tax (about 1p off the standard rate) the increase in spending power from the tax cut will lead to the creation of just over 20,000 new jobs, working out at close to £50,000 a job. If, however, this same £1 billion is used to increase current public spending on items such as education or health care or local government, 65,000 new jobs will result, an average of £15,000 a job. Extra spending on infrastructure, at £26,000 a job, would create 38,000 jobs. And, in the bargain basement, spending that extra £1 billion on special employment measures, such as the Community Programme, could lead to a cut in unemployment of close to 500,000 people. Cutting value added tax or the employers' national insurance contributions are even less effective in job-creation than income tax cuts. In short, then, if a

Table 8.2: Cost per person removed from unemployment, £ per annum

Tax cuts	£
Income tax	47,000
Value added tax	58,800
Employers' national insurance contributions	59,200
Public infrastructure investment	
Health	51,000
Education	26,200
Roads	32,700
Dwellings	15,800
Other	27,800
Average	26,200
Current public expenditure	
Defence	45,200
Health	10,700
Other central government	20,400
Education and local government	10,400
Average	15,300
Special employment measures	
Community Programme	2,200
Enterprise Allowance Scheme	2,650
Job Release Scheme	1,650
Youth Training Scheme	1,400
Young (New) Workers Scheme	2,400
Average	2,050

Note: 1984–5 prices. PSBR cost (government borrowing).
Source: Davies G. and Metcalf D.H. (1985), 'Generating jobs', *The Economics Analyst*, April.

government is at all interested in reducing unemployment then the way to do it in the least effective way possible is to cut taxes. In his March 1987 Budget, Chancellor Nigel Lawson reduced the standard rate of income tax by 2p in the £, to 27p, at a cost of £2.2 billion. The 1988 Budget is likely to bring a further reduction, possibly to the magic 25p. These changes, at a cost of £4.4 billion, will cut unemployment by just 80,000.

The London Business School (LBS) confirm that as a way of tackling unemployment, income tax cuts are the worst option.

Table 8.3: Cut in unemployment per £1 billion of borrowing[a]

£1 billion spent on:	Number of people
Income tax	21,300
Value Added Tax	17,000
Employers' national insurance	16,900
Public investment	38,200
Current public spending	65,400
Special employment measures	487,800

Note: a. Public Sector Borrowing Requirement (PSBR).
Source: As Table 8.2.

Their own estimates show that a £2-billion cut in income tax reduces unemployment by just 20,000 in the first year and 58,000 by the end of year two. Tax cuts raise consumer spending and stimulate imports. A general rise in government spending of £2 billion would cut unemployment by 240,000 over two years. Spending measures targeted at the long-term unemployed would have an even bigger impact. The best buy from the LBS is to use the £2 billion *not* to take 2p off income tax, but to expand special employment measures. In the first year alone, the LBS estimate that this could cut unemployment by 300,000.

Table 8.2 shows the calculations made by Davies and Metcalf on the cost per person removed from unemployment. Table 8.3 gives an indication of the cut in unemployment that results from an extra £1 billion in government borrowing, spent in the ways included in the table. Naturally, cost per job on infrastructure spending is higher than most elements in current spending (e.g. salaries, consumables). This is because of the construction, equipment and other capital costs over and above the labour costs involved. Defence comes high per new job on current spending because of the training and the kitting-out requirements of soldiers and sailors. Conscription is not a cheap solution to unemployment!

We know with some accuracy, then, just what the costs of relieving the crisis of unemployment will be. All that is required is for the government of the day to put a return to full employment back again at the top of its economic and political agenda. Instead of using high unemployment as a means of deflating the economy and a whip for the backs of the trade unions, the personal and national costs of having 4 million unemployed just have to be recognised. Unless this is done we are passing a sentence of idleness and poverty, at best, and a death sentence at worst on millions of our fellow citizens and their children. The opportunity to cut unemployment is there for the grasping.

9. Cutting Unemployment in the 1990s: Back to 3 Per Cent

The task is huge: a return to 3 per cent unemployment by the mid-1990s. If we take 4 million unemployed as our starting-point, then the objective has to be to find work for over 3 million people. The initial targets have to be the long-term unemployed, the young unemployed, those living in the highest-unemployment parts of the UK, including the inner cities, and those formerly at work in unskilled and semi-skilled jobs, particularly in manufacturing industry. A number of policy initiatives can help many of these different groups simultaneously.

Work still needs to be carried out on the supply-side, with action required for some of the present unemployed on the quality and price of labour. Employers have a marked reluctance to recruit the long-term unemployed to vacancies, so some incentives on labour costs are necessary so that employers will positively discriminate in favour of those without jobs for long periods. Those with redundant skills, or with job experience where the jobs will continue to decline, have to be equipped with skills that meet the labour-market needs of today and tomorrow. Job subsidies of some kind, and training and retraining schemes will continue to play a part in the move to a fully employed UK. There is also socially useful community work that still needs to be done, now more than ever. The 'public squalor and private affluence' debates of the past have returned to the UK with more force than ever. Direct public-sector job-creation in a range of services and industries, rather than make-work on special schemes, has to be planned for.

But the job subsidies and training initiatives proposed in detail below will be to little good effect unless the demand for labour is also stimulated. As noted elsewhere in this book, up to three-quarters of the rise in unemployment in the UK results from a deficiency in demand in the economy. It is just no good putting unemployed people through training schemes without ensuring that the jobs for which they are being trained materialise on successful completion of vocational training. In this sense, existing government-sponsored training such as the Youth or Job Training Schemes perpetrate a con on the unemployed. Targeted spending on infrastructure and on particular public services would stimulate the demand for labour by both private- and public-sector employing organisations. We need reminding that the demand for labour is a derived demand—in the absence of an increased demand for the goods and services produced by labour there is no good reason for thinking that employers would choose to take on more staff. We have to tickle that demand in a directed way to create jobs for those shouldering the burden of unemployment. We can get unemployment down to 1 million by 1995.

YOUTH UNEMPLOYMENT

The UK has one of the least-well-trained workforces in the industrialised world. On average, private employers spend just 0.15 per cent of turnover a year on training their workforces, amounting to a puny £200 a year per employee. This compares very unfavourably with the Federal Republic of Germany, the USA, Japan and France. Training for the future at all levels has to be improved: initial training for young people and updating and retraining throughout their working lives for older workers. We currently permit young people to quit full-time education at age 16 and go into a job (if they are lucky) where there may be no training whatsoever. This cannot continue. No person under the age of 18 should be in a job where there is not a substantial amount of vocational and life-skills training. The answer is not to make the existing Youth Training Scheme compulsory, but rather to think again about the needs for the future of young people themselves and of the labour market.

Legislation is required to impose a minimum education and training leaving age (METLA) of 18 years. From the age of 14 to 18 young people can be continuing their studies in school or college full-time, or they could be engaging in off- and on-the-job training with an employer or a training consortium. A break from full-time education could take place at any time from age 14 onwards, provided that the recipient organisation is contracted to a new National Training Scheme (NTS) to provide validated training representing 40 per cent minimum of a trainee's time each year. Nationwide schemes such as the Technical and Vocational Education Initiative (TVEI) already cross the age bridge from 14 to 18. Some existing youth training schemes (with amendment) would offer a satisfactory placement for young people. The Certificate of Pre-Vocational Education (CPVE) is already in place, as are a number of other college-based schemes of work, education and training.

At present, the minimum school-leaving age is 16. Thereafter young people can stay on full time at school or college, and receive no financial assistance whatsoever. They can take a job, few of which offer training. They can join YTS and receive £28.50 a week, or in 1987 they can remain unemployed and receive benefit, but not for 1988 onwards. In future all young people over the age of 16, whether they opt for the education or vocational training route should receive £30 a week for the first year, and £35 a week for the second year. In the year of introduction, when education and training allowances (ETA) would be paid to all 16-year-olds, the cost would be just under £2 billion, less existing expenditure on YTS allowances and supplementary benefit. When up and running for 16- to 18-year-olds, the costs of allowances would be £2.5 billion a year net.

The existing financial support for 16- and 17-year-olds distorts choice (and the labour market), encouraging early leaving from school and college. Neutralising this disincentive effect by a universal payment and compulsory participation in education or vocational training to the age of 18, is a forward-looking measure that is certain to dramatically improve the skills of young people, enhance productivity and economic growth and lead to much better opportunities in the labour market.

For those not staying on in school or college after the ages of 14 or 15 or 16, vocational and life-skills training would take place for a minimum of two days in a week or, if organised as block training, 20 weeks each year in total. Local consortia, under the auspices of the Manpower Services Commission (Training Commission), and involving local employers and Chambers of Commerce, local education authorities, training agencies, the careers service, trade unions and educationalists, would issue contracts to those providing training schemes for 14–18-year-olds. A £1500-a-year training payment for each place approved would go to the contractor. The consortia would expect training programmes to take account of local and regional labour-market conditions, and would receive advice on trends in labour demand and supply from the MSC and external advisors. In this way, training could be organised for young people that would attempt to match skills acquisition with employer demands up to five years ahead. Resource-allocation decisions would reside with the Local Training Consortium (LTC), but there would be nothing to stop schools and colleges bidding for funds to run schemes themselves.

For youth unemployment, then, the proposal is for:

(1) a minimum education and training leaving age (METLA) of 18 years;

(2) from the age of 14, young people could leave full-time education provided they joined an approved vocational training scheme;

(3) a new National Training Scheme would be established: part of its responsibility would be to establish Local Training Consortia (LTC) that would approve bids to run training for 14- to 18-year-olds;

(4) for those not in full-time education, at least 40 per cent of the trainee's time would be spent in off-the-job vocational and life-skills training, the remainder would be work experience and on-the-job training;

(5) all young people over the age of 16 would receive an Education and Training Allowance (ETA), £30 in the first year and £35 in the second year. This allowance would be paid whether teenagers opted for continued full-time education or vocational training. A trainee allowance would not be paid to those under 16 years of age, but vocational training and other expenses would be paid;

(6) organisers of training would be paid £1500 a year per approved place;

(7) employing organisations with more than 25 employees, and *not* providing any training places themselves or work experience for participating teenagers, would have to pay a *training levy*. This would amount to £1500 a year for every ten employees.

This is a forward-looking proposal to counter existing deficiencies in youth training, including YTS, and is a positive response to youth unemployment. Immediate action should be taken to implement the proposals.

LONG-TERM UNEMPLOYMENT

Those who have been out of work for a year or longer are the most disadvantaged in today's labour market. Existing assistance for them takes the form of special measures such as the Community Programme, or the Jobstart Allowance (paid to the employee). According to official statistics, 1.3 million people have been unemployed for over a year, and the real figure certainly exceeds 1.5 million. This is the group who need the most urgent attention.

During a period of extended unemployment, work habits (for those who have worked before) are forgotten, any skills become unused, and the experience of unemployment itself is debilitating. Employers have an antithesis to recruiting the long-term unemployed. Together with the demand stimulation measures discussed below, a combination of job subsidy and training can assist enormously. Employers do need a particular incentive to recruit the long-term unemployed. The incentive should be generous. Each unemployed person currently costs the state £6000 in a full year. A massive return to work on the part of the long-term unemployed can be almost costless.

The first proposal is that every person who has been unemployed for a year or longer receives a book of long-term unemployment vouchers (LTUV). An employer recruiting somebody who has been out of work for this length of time to a full-time job can cash in these vouchers and receive a subsidy of £80 a week. This is paid to the employer regardless of the wages of the recruit. This is a matter for the employer and employee. As soon as an unemployed person hits the 12-month mark on his or her unemployment record, receipt of the job subsidy is automatic.

In order to prevent the 'churning' of employees, sacking some in order to take advantage of the LTUV job subsidy, and then perhaps going through the process again on the expiry of the vouchers, there have to be some conditions attached. The recruitment should be incremental, in the sense that to use the LTUV the employer must be employing more people than 12 months previously. The £80-a-week subsidy is attached to a particular individual, and the vouchers can only be cashed in for that person for each week of employment. This particular job subsidy will last for three years from the date of employment, permitting employers to make medium-term plans on labour costs and manpower requirements.

The LTUV scheme should be introduced immediately for all those unemployed for a year or more. It is difficult to gauge the impact of such a scheme in the short term, but with improved training and selected expansion in the economy, it is expected that few long-term unemployed people wanting a job will be unable to find one. It is also proposed that the LTUV should have a differential value for areas with especially high unemployment and for particularly hard-hit groups. Voucher values of £100 and £120 should be experimented with where registered unemployment in a travel-to-work area exceeds 14 per cent at the time of introduction, or where there is a high ratio of unemployment to vacancies, or where high unemployment is experienced in small zones of the inner cities. The unemployed disabled should receive the high-value voucher after a six-month period. The higher-value subsidy should be paid to employers for 12 months, and for the following two years the jobs subsidy would revert to £80 per week. If such a scheme were to be introduced there could be a good opportunity for experimenting with different values in different localities and to tweak the LTUV scheme to make it most effective.

A job subsidy of £80, £100 and £120 per week sounds enormous. However, apart from administration, this supply-side measure working on the labour costs of a particularly disenfranchised group, is virtually self-funding. The costs of unemployment are now so enormous, with the direct costs of benefit together with taxation and national insurance foregone amounting to £120 a week on average, that we can afford to use job subsidies in this way.

No employer, whether in manufacturing or services, whether public or private, and regardless of location or size, will be excluded from being able to use the LTUV scheme in recruitment. All long-term unemployed people over the age of 18 are eligible. Its impact will be large. Of course, not all long-term unemployed people will use the LTUV scheme, and even with such a subsidy will remain unattractive as employees. Training and retraining can help to compensate for this.

The existing Community Programme scheme should be quickly phased out. In its stead the new National Training Scheme would set about combining work experience and vocational and life-skills training (including labour-market re-entry training) for all those unemployed for 12 months and longer. Initially, 500,000 places would be provided. The work experience involved might well include community work of various kinds, along the lines of some of the better Community Programme schemes, but all would have a pattern of two days a week training of various kinds, depending on the interests and abilities of participants and local labour-market conditions. A sub-group of the Local Training Consortium involving local authority, employer association and trade union representatives would be responsible for approving proposals and for monitoring progress. Those bidding for funds to organise such training would have to demonstrate that the training provided would have a direct impact on the employability of participants, and would have to take labour-market trends into account. As with the National Training Scheme for 14- to 18-year-olds, training for the adult unemployed cannot be permitted to teach yesterday's skills.

Unemployed people taking part in NTS would receive a taxable training allowance of £100 per week, whilst retaining eligibility for other benefit payments that depend on personal circumstances. The allowance to those organising training schemes and work experience would be £1500 a year. The normal duration of training schemes would be 12 months, but extension to a maximum three years would be in order subject to satisfactory monitoring and progress reports. The intention must be to extend NTS to those unemployed for shorter periods.

The net cost of providing 500,000 places for the long-term unemployed on NTS would be under £1.5 billion. Again, public and private employers, training agencies, voluntary organisations and educational institutions would all be eligible to bid for support.

Even with generous job subsidies to employers, and a revitalised and forward-looking NTS for the long-term unemployed, and even with a selective expansion of the economy aimed specifically at unemployed groups, it is at least possible that some long-term unemployed people will remain excluded for one reason or another. As we have seen elsewhere, the experience of unemployment saps individuals' motivations and interests in a whole variety of ways. Provision may need to be made for the group of long-term unemployed people still not participating in full-time employment with the help of the LTUV, or working to achieve full-time employment with NTS. What is required is an employer and trainer of last resort.

It is proposed that local authorities be funded to establish local centres of a new UK Employment Scheme. Without time limits on participation these would be jobs of direct benefit to the local community, as are many existing Community Programme jobs, but participants would be involved in personal- and social-skills training, and where remedial tuition could be given if necessary, for example on literacy and numeracy. It is anticipated that once the LTUV subsidy and NTS measures are up and fully running, the demand for places of the UK Employment Scheme would be relatively low. Initially, planning and funding should provide for 200,000 places, unevenly distributed regionally to take account of different unemployment rates. Local authorities setting up units for the UK Employment Scheme would receive earmarked funding for it through the central government support grant system. Participants would receive £80 a week initially, uprated each year in line with the cost of living, without a time limit on participation. The net cost of providing 200,000 places on this basis would not be so very different from *per capita* Community Programme provision and would be just over £500 million in total. Participation would be compulsory.

Unemployed people themselves do not always recognise the massively adverse effects the experience of unemployment has on them and their families. The personal and national costs of unemployment, in terms of physical and mental health as well as in terms of poverty, deprivation and lost output, is so large and the consequences so severe that they are not always recognised or appreciated by the unemployed themselves. Incentives would be provided through the jobs subsidy and NTS. The expansion of employment organised through increased public spending would make jobs for the unemployed much more plentiful. In the last resort employment would be guaranteed through the UK Employment Scheme. No person should remain without employment or labour-market-orientated training for more than a year. Long-term unemployment cannot be permitted to exist, and if this does require compulsion for the small number remaining after the satisfactory implementation of all the new policies to relieve the crisis of unemployment, then participation has to be compulsory.

For the long-term unemployed then, a range of specific and effective changes are proposed here:

(1) a jobs subsidy should be introduced for all people unemployed for a year or longer. It would take the form of a Long Term Unemployment Voucher (LTUV) worth £80-per-week minimum to an employer recruiting the long-term unemployed;

(2) all long-term unemployed people would be eligible for the vouchers after 12 months on the dole;

(3) the subsidy would be paid to the employer provided the number of employees at work in the organisation was greater than a year previously;

(4) no type of employer would be excluded from the scheme. Manufacturing and services, public and private, would all be eligible;

(5) the jobs subsidy voucher would be 'attached' to a specific individual, and the subsidy could be claimed for up to three years;

(6) higher-value LTUVs would be used for particularly disadvantaged groups and for those in the highest unemployment regions, including the inner cities;

(7) it is proposed that a LTUV of £100 and £120 a week is appropriate for 12 months for such individuals, with the following two years at the standard £80 subsidy. Experimentation should take place in different parts of the country with different value vouchers for such individuals and groups;

(8) the new National Training Scheme (NTS) should provide 500,000 places for the long-term unemployed, involving work experience and two days a week off-the-job training;

(9) participation of the long-term unemployed on the scheme would normally be 12 months, with a maximum three years;

(10) those taking part would receive a training allowance of £100 a week, with the training-scheme sponsors receiving £1500 per place;

(11) a local-authority based UK Employment Scheme would be established as an employer of last resort for the long-term unemployed;

(12) funding for the UK Employment Scheme would come, earmarked, through the central government support grant, with

participants receiving £80 a week and retaining eligibility to claim other benefits that are dependent on personal circumstances;

(13) the UK Employment Scheme would provide community-based employment for those not finding jobs with the assistance of the jobs-subsidising LTUVs and not undergoing training with NTS;

(14) initially the UK Employment Scheme would provide 200,000 places but would expand or contract according to need;

(15) participation for those not finding jobs and not on NTS would be compulsory;

(16) the total net cost of these measures aimed at the relief of long-term unemployment would be under £2.5 billion.

UNEMPLOYMENT IN THE REGIONS

In the past regional policy has favoured aid that attempted to bring work to the workers. In the form applied, in the main it failed, with too little account being taken of the net job-creation effects of different kinds of grant aid. Even worse, many companies have been able to use government assistance in the depressed regions in a way that helped them to sack people. A combination of policies is needed that would both encourage the growth of employment in the regions of the UK *and* assist in taking workers to the work.

Clearly, the LTUV proposal is going to help, particularly if those out of work in the country's unemployment blackspots possess a higher-value voucher. The National Training Scheme and the development of the UK Employment Scheme are also, by definition, going to benefit most those areas currently most adversely affected by unemployment. Other steps can be taken.

A national insurance 'holiday' should be made available to employers expanding their workforces where unemployment is high. While the employees themselves would continue to pay their own contributions, the employer's national insurance contributions should be waived for 12 months where the recruitment of an unemployed person takes place. This would reduce labour costs in the regions over and above the use of a LTUV for the recruitment of the long-term unemployed. The national insurance 'holiday' would be available whatever the duration of registered unemployment. The only requirement would be that an increase in the total number of employees was taking place.

As with the LTUV, this policy would skew job-market opportunities in favour of the unemployed and against job changers. I make no apologies for this: it is necessary. After the 12-month expiry period, provided that the workforce was stable or growing, but certainly not declining, the employer's national insurance contribution would be paid at one-half of the normal rate for a further two years before coming into line with that levied in lower-unemployment regions. A combination of a higher value LTUV job subsidy in high-unemployment parts of the UK, together with zero national insurance contributions for growing employers, would make expansion attractive. Incoming, mobile and relocating enterprises would also be looking closely at such benefits, since the costs of labour to the employer would be so low.

Urban Development Corporations, Enterprise Zones, City Action Teams, Inner City Partnerships and Inner Cities Task Force Units have all been assisting in the regions and the southern inner cities. A greater involvement of the local communities and local government is necessary to make the most of the opportunities presented by these kinds of initiative. In the main, their budgets are very low, limiting their effectiveness, apart from the bulldozing briefs of the Development Corporations in such areas as London's Docklands and Merseyside, where local involvement is virtually non-existent. A total of twelve Urban Development Corporations in all are scheduled to be working on the problems of urban decay and dereliction. Seven ministries are involved in the amelioration of regional and innter-city problems. Urban Development Corporations are now necessary for many more cities and towns than the twelve that have been designated. But their decision-making structure needs drastic overhauling, to bring in the local authorities, representatives of employer and employee associations, and most critically, the local community. With better structures and bigger budgets, and much more numerous, Urban Development Corporations on this basis remove the need for the Inner City Task Force Units, and Enterprise Zones and the rest. The sixteen Task Forces, under the auspices of the Department of Trade and Industry, have a budget of just £18 million. The tightly boundaried Enterprise Zones have created extra jobs, sometimes leading to spectacular reductions in registered unemployment within the zone. Overall, however, 60 per cent of the jobs created have gone to those living outside the Enterprise Zone area. Some 55 Inner City Partnerships spread money even more thinly around for local community projects, but at least there is local involvement. Revamped and more extensive Urban Development Corporations involving all the groups noted above could make a massive contribution to relieving high unemployment in the urban areas, including, of course, the regions. It also would remove the confusion, lack of coordination and, at times, 'Big Brother' decision-making that is just so apparent at present. The Royal Institute of British Architects (RIBA) has called the different initiatives 'a confusing, frustrating web of bureaucracy'.

RIBA have also called for the creation of an Urban Renewal Agency with a £25-billion budget over five years. Just half a billion pounds are currently being spent from public funds in urban regeneration, in spite of the plight of the inner cities reportedly going to the top of the government agenda for action. There are no plans to inject new funds of any consequence into the inner cities and the high-unemployment regions. The new Urban Development Corporations proposed above should share a budget of at least £2 billion a year—four times more than is currently being spent. To this, of course, must be added the extra infrastructure expenditure detailed below, much of which would take place in urban areas. If the experience of the existing Development Corporations is any guide, private money will also follow public funding into the cities. The scale of private money in London Docklands will not be repeated anywhere else, however.

The regional problem is not only concerned with urban decay, of course. New Regional Development Corporations in high-unemployment regions should also enjoy some of the tax and business-rating benefits of existing Enterprise Zones. The main goal has to be the generation of new jobs, but if the creation of Urban and Regional Development Corporations results in some redistribution of jobs from high-employment to high-unemployment parts of the country, then we should not be too upset about such an eventuality. The Regional Development Corporations would have the power to make grants and loans to start up and incoming employers. Local government at all levels, trade unions, local employers and, once again, representatives of the non-urban communities should all be involved in decision-making on resource allocation.

All of the measures discussed above are, as before, attempts to bring work to the unemployed workers in the regions and in the cities nationwide. If there are unemployed people in, say, high-unemployment Liverpool who desire to move to, say, full-employment Crawley, then proper assistance has to be made available to enable these workers to move to the work. A Job Search Allowance, and the reimbursement of necessary expenses involved in job search should be available to all unemployed people who require them. A maximum two-week travel period at any one time would be available at usual benefit levels (for the individuals) plus 20 per cent. Assistance with the transfer costs would also be available, regardless of the donor or recipient region, for those who are successful in finding work outside their home areas. Clearly, a much better information base in Jobcentres is required, but a two-week period can be considered reasonable for an initial search.

However, it has been demonstrated so many times in the mid-1980s that finding and accepting a job is not enough. There are other inhibitors of mobility, the most serious of which is housing. Acute shortages of housing to rent, exacerbated by the sale of council housing, has led to labour mobility being especially difficult in the 1980s. Council-house transfer applications have tended to show a pronounced flow away from high-unemployment regions. But, of course, for an application to become, in reality, a move, a flow of a similar scale is required in the other direction. Not surprisingly, this has not been happening. In areas where job opportunities are more plentiful, private accommodation to rent is in highest demand and commands the highest rents. As the ranks of the unemployed contain a disproportionate number of unskilled and semi-skilled workers, where they do find work outside their home area, the wages and salaries paid will frequently be below the average for the recipient area. A job there may be for some, but housing, if it is available at all, is at rents beyond the reach of the mobile worker.

Public spending on housing has been cut in half since 1979. The council-house building programme has all but collapsed, and council-housing stock has been sold at a discount to tenants, often people who may have become owner-occupiers in any case, even without the housing-privatisation programme. In its own right housing policy is in a state of chaos and crisis: it also impacts upon the ability of those searching for work to be mobile.

One part of the infrastructure investment programme has to be in housing (see below). Not only does this create jobs for unemployed construction workers and the unskilled and semi-skilled from manufacturing, but it also can assist with labour mobility. A public-housing investment programme has to be launched without delay. Most of the existing 4 million unfit houses are in London or the northern industrial towns. New council-house building should start as a means of job-creation, but also to provide accommodation for incoming employees. In areas of high employment there is a particular dearth of available housing to rent. Investment in council housing is the answer, and in planning housing provision for the future, labour-market forecasts will play a crucial role. It may seem odd that special attention should be given to council-house building in areas where employment is currently very high. Forward-looking investment in infrastructure of all kinds has to take account of where the demand for labour is going to be highest and take steps to meet this demand. In the absence of national manpower planning and the state direction of companies and of employees, infrastructure investment has to deal with the UK as we find it. Local authorities in the south do have long and growing housing waiting lists, there are many people in the more depressed regions wanting employment opportunities, and there are employers already experiencing labour shortages. A growth of council housing in areas of low unemployment can assist all these groups. During the course of construction, of course, 'migrant' construction workers will almost certainly need to be brought in. Some may even stay to live in the houses they have built.

The availability and price of rented accommodation is not the only impediment to labour mobility caused by housing-policy confusion and the vagaries of the market place. Differences in the purchase price of owner-occupied dwellings too can make it extremely difficult for people to move to jobs. The phasing out of mortgage-interest relief would leave more tax revenue for the Treasury to allocate to council-housing investment. It might also slow down, stop or reverse the growing house-price differences in different parts of the country. More even and much lower unemployment would also have this effect. A contrary effect is likely to be felt when domestic rates are replaced by a poll tax or community charge. In the absence of a tax on housing, property prices will increase by over 5 per cent. This will stretch the already mighty cash gap between houses prices in London and the south-east and other parts of the country. It is also time to introduce capital gains tax on the appreciation of house values. Not politically popular (neither is the abandonment of mortgage-interest relief) but a necessary change: nevertheless, it would raise £3 billion a year at the moment.

Other than by effectively reducing unemployment in the regions, and thus boosting incomes and the local economies, in the short term probably little can be done about the differential price of housing. However, an increased availability of affordable housing to rent would make low regional house prices less of an inhibitor of labour mobility. And property taxation on capital gains would assist in dampening down the differences.

This section on regional unemployment and the problems of the inner cities has been wide in scope. The main proposals to assist the high unemployment parts of the country are:

(1) The LTUV, which provides a job subsidy to employers, would be worth up to 50 per cent more in areas of high unemployment;
(2) Because of regional differences in unemployment and available jobs, the initiatives proposed for the NTS and the UK Employment Scheme are bound to assist most in areas of high unemployment;
(3) In high-unemployment areas, employers would pay no national insurance contributions for a year for new workers recruited from the dole queue, provided their workforce was expanding;
(4) After the 12-month national insurance 'holiday', the employers' contribution would be levied at one-half of the proper rate for a further two years;
(5) New Urban Development Corporations would be established for all major towns and cities with urban blight or high unemployment;

(6) The Urban Development Corporations would fully involve the local communities, local government and employer and employee associations in their decision-making;

(7) £2 billion in the first instance would be made available to the Urban Development Corporations, this is four times the amount currently spent on the inner citites;

(8) All other existing urban initiatives would be cancelled;

(9) New Regional Development Corporations would be established in non-urban, high-unemployment areas, with a brief to stimulate regeneration and create jobs;

(10) A Job Search Allowance (JSA) would be available to all unemployed people looking for work outside their home area. The JSA would pay unemployed people 20 per cent above their usual weekly benefit level, for a maximum two weeks at any one time. Necessary travel, accommodation and other expenses would also be paid;

(11) Labour mobility would also be assisted by the construction of more council housing, particularly in areas of high employment and where affordable accommodation is in short supply;

(12) A large expansion of council housing and the refurbishment of unfit dwellings would assist mobility: it also creates jobs for construction workers and the less skilled unemployed;

(13) Taxation reform on housing mortgage interest relief and capital gains would assist in the evening-up of house prices: low unemployment would also have this effect.

INCREASED PUBLIC SPENDING

Council-house waiting lists are long and growing. Four million houses in this country are unfit for human habitation, or require £7000 or more spent on them to bring up to a reasonable standard. Sewers collapse regularly in many of our large cities and towns. There is a backlog of planned road-improvement schemes waiting for finance to become available. Road maintenance has been squeezed. Many of our 5-year-olds still attend primary schools that were built for their great grandparents or even earlier. The hospital-rebuilding programme needs accelerating. Our prisons are unfit and overcrowded.

There is certainly no shortage of vital infrastructure tasks to be done. There are also 4 million unemployed people who can make a massive contribution to these tasks but who are currently idle. The question has been asked before: who can deny the simple logic of bringing these tasks and the people together to do them? As we saw in Chapter 8, there is close to £100 billion worth of infrastructure work that now urgently needs undertaking. The years of Thatcherite neglect have certainly taken their toll here, as in the length of the dole queue.

In housing construction and refurbishment in the public sector 250,000 jobs should be created straight away. In a full year this would cost £3.5 billion. Additional earmarked funding should be channelled through local authorities and the housing associations in order for this necessary building work to be set in motion. A further 250,000 jobs should come in other infrastructure projects, such as school and hospital renewal, sewerage and water-pipe replacements, prison rebuilding and road programmes. In the main, projects of this kind are more expensive per job created than investment in housing, and are certainly more expensive than simply recruiting to the public services such as health and welfare. This part of the capital-investment programme would cost £6 billion. It is expensive in terms of short-term costs, but the benefits to the nation would accrue over a period of 25 years and more. Any investment decision has to balance these longer-term benefits and their real value against the current costs required to complete a worthwhile and profitable project. This is what our captains of industry do all the time. We should not shirk from the short-term costs in such decisions, since benefits come from reduced unemployment now and an improved infrastructure into the twenty-first century. And one further aspect of this should be noted. Targeted expansion of public spending on infrastructure in this way reaps benefits for the private sector too, stimulating activity (and profits) and creating jobs there as well.

Increased spending to raise the quality of central and local government services would also be money well spent. Our public services are hard pressed. Reduced resources and sharply increased workloads have been particular features of the 1980s. Again it is more than just sensible to bring together the tasks that need to be done with unemployed people wanting to do them. Playgroup and nursery education provision in this country is in scarce supply. The number of elderly people in the population is growing rapidly, requiring additional services ranging from ancillary workers in hospitals, home-helps, and care assistants in residential homes to ambulance drivers. A total of 500,000 new jobs in health, education and local government services would cost £5 billion a year. From park attendants and gardeners, to road sweepers and refuse collectors, from playtime supervisors in schools to playgroup assistants, the jobs are there to be done. Let us do them.

Clearly, it can be seen that a major element in the public-spending programme involves an increase of 1 million in direct public employment in a range of infrastructure and public-service activities. These are real jobs. And just as real are the estimated minimum 500,000 jobs that will be generated in private-sector employing organisations as a result of the public-sector orders for materials and equipment involved, and the increased spending power of the newly employed public-service workers of different kinds.

Now increases in public employment have not always had the enormous benefit to the unemployed anticipated. We do need to have some idea of the impact of such measures on employment in the private sector, the encouragement given to even more people to enter the labour market and on wage costs. Without careful planning, targeting and conditions attached, increased public employment may merely have the effect of bringing into employment those unemployed people who would have found jobs in any case.

Central government is going to be providing extra funding to local authorities, some central spending departments and other organisations in anticipation that the £14.5 billion increase in spending on infrastructure and improved public services will be used to further an unemployment-alleviation objective. It cannot be left to chance, since there is sometimes a clear mismatch in public-employment expansion between objectives and delivery. If past experience is any guide, and there are also lessons to be learnt here from other countries, including France, the additional finance made available could well be used to fund public-employment expansion that was going to take place in any case, even in the absence of new money. We also have to be aware of a potential displacement effect, meaning that those recruited through public-spending initiatives might displace existing workers or those who would otherwise have been appointed. Research work in the late 1970s by Johnson and Tomola suggests that for every 100 extra jobs in public employment funded in this way, the net increase in jobs is between 50 and 70.

Another potential weakness is that newly created vacancies in the public sector might be filled by groups with good employment prospects elsewhere, leaving high-unemployment groups still idle. Increased public spending as a means of cutting the dole queue just has to be spent on those jobs requiring unskilled and semi-skilled workers, aimed at those experiencing the highest incidence of unemployment. These jobs also tend to be more lowly paid, so a given increase in public spending actually buys you more jobs, which is important.

In order for infrastructure and public-service projects to gain approval for the new money, it would have to be clearly demonstrated that this is new work, going well beyond existing funded plans, that a net increase in employment on some scale is in prospect, and that a high proportion of those taken on to do the work will have to come from the ranks of the unemployed. The extra public spending has to be used for job-creation, and it would not be permitted to use any of it to provide better financial rewards for those already in employment. Since very few of the jobs involved will be high-pay, high-skill ones, the effects on wage expectations elsewhere should be minimal. With such an excess supply of labour in existence at present capable of carrying out these tasks, little sleep should be lost over wage inflation.

The double benefit is that the increase in public-sector orders and increased spending power associated with a sharp rise in employment will also create jobs in the private sector throughout the economy. And this type of public-employment expansion, with the projects selected, will feed through almost exclusively to UK companies. Unlike general expansionary policies which have been suggested by some, the demand for home-produced goods, services, materials and equipment will be particularly stimulated. The extra money spent will create jobs in the UK and not abroad.

Increased public spending, then, has to be targeted on those infra-structure projects that can make most use of the skills of the unemployed, while at the same time making a strong contribution to clearing up the backlog of infrastructure decay that has been permitted to advance in the 1980s. Improving the quality of services too must have in its sights the jobs that most need to be done, while making full use of unemployed workers. The public-spending programme, in brief, involves:

(1) creating 250,000 jobs in housing construction, repair and renovation in the public sector, at a cost of £3.5 billion a year;
(2) a further 250,000 jobs for unemployed construction, semi-skilled and unskilled workers in school and hospital renewal and refurbishment, sewerage and water-pipe replacement, prison rebuilding and road-improvement programmes. This would cost £6 billion a year;
(3) 500,000 new jobs in the public services to improve their quality and in order to develop new services; particular areas of expansion to include ancillary workers in schools and hospitals, home-helps, care assistants and local government manual workers. These jobs would cost £5 billion;
(4) these extra 1 million jobs in public employment would bring in their wake more than 500,000 jobs in the private sector as a result of increased orders for materials and equipment and the increased spending power of newly employed workers;
(5) bids for using the new money (£14.5 billion in total) would be required to demonstrate that the main job-creation benefits would go to the unemployed.

TIMING, COST AND PAYING FOR THE PROGRAMME

The infrastructure and public-services expansion programmes would need to be built up over a three-year period. Much planning and background work needs to be undertaken before full implementation. Such a growth in public (and private) employment would be difficult to absorb in one go, so a phased introduction involving expenditure of £5 billion in year one, £10 billion in year two and the full £14.5 billion in the third year is proposed. The policies outlined on infrastructure and public services should be built into public-spending plans for a full five-year period, on a rolling-forward basis. In this way the transition from mass unemployment to full employment can be eased, and proper funding can be organised. A build-up of activity, commencing in, say, 1990, would ensure the creation of up to 2 million new public- and private- sector jobs by 1995 from investment in infrastructure and public services. This must be our aim.

For the long-term unemployed, half a million of whom have already been out of work for three years or longer, there can be no delay. The proposed LTUV jobs subsidy should be introduced straight away, at its standard value and enhanced value for high-unemployment areas. Work on developing a National Training Scheme for the unemployed and for 14- to 18-year-olds needs to commence immediately. Local authorities should be invited to prepare plans to participate in the UK Employment Scheme. The crisis of unemployment is of such proportions that work does need to commence straight away on planning for a return to full employment by 1995.

The cost of all the programmes outlined in this chapter amount to £24 billion in a full year, when fully implemented. This includes £4 billion for implementation of the 18-years minimum education and training leaving age, the allowance for 16- to 18-year-olds and the development of a National Training Scheme for young people and the unemployed; £4 billion for the new Urban and Regional Development Corporations; £9.5 billion on housing investment and other infrastructure work; and a further £5 billion a year for an expansion of public services. This sounds like a lot of money. It is a lot of money.

However, it should be remembered that public spending in 1988–9 will amount to just under £160 billion. Even if it were possible to introduce all the back-to-work programmes simultaneously and immediately (which it is not) the £24-billion total increase in spending represents a 15 per cent rise on existing government expenditure. We should aim to have introduced all measures within a three-year period, so the build-up of spending will be much more gradual.

Very importantly, we should also remember that unemployment itself is now costing the country some £20 billion, in the form of benefits paid, and taxation, national insurance and production foregone. High employment leads to much lower spending in the social security budget and higher receipts to the Treasury in the form of income tax, value added tax and corporation tax. Certainly, initial and substantial job-creating, pump-priming money has to be found, but as other costs fall and government receipts rise, the *net* cost of the measures becomes less than half of a gross cost. In public-spending planning we can provide for a £24-billion increase in spending to pave the road to full employment, but the social security budget can be reduced by £5 billion in part-compensation as a result of the fewer jobless having to be paid benefit. And year by year the government's revenue account will reap the rewards of back-to-work policies.

Before considering just how the increased initial spending is to be financed, a small number of other salient points must be mentioned. First, a reminder that unemployment itself is costing the country £6000 a year for each unemployed person. Second, the costings in this chapter are, if anything, pessimistic. No favours are done if there is a deliberate underestimate of the costs of implementing a full-employment programme. Plucking numbers out of the air and halving them to try to convince the population (electorate and policy-makers alike) that full employment can be had on the cheap is simply unhelpful. In the medium term high employment does come close to being self-funding, it is true, but in the short term sustainable job-creation is expensive. Third, throughout this book the figure of 4 million unemployed has been taken as a guide. How much easier it would be if we could accept the official unemployment count of 2.9 million or so and operate accordingly. To return to 3 per cent unemployment requires the creation of over 3 million jobs, using a variety of methods. We just cannot use the official count when it suits us in curing the crisis of unemployment, but use proper estimates of the real scale of the unemployment mountain when trying to take pot shots at government policy and their blatant manipulation of statistics. Fourth, and significantly, we also have to consider seriously in any policy decisions the personal and national costs of unemployment that are non-pecuniary in nature. Any half-decent economist in assessing the costs and benefits of full employment policies, should take into account those costs that are not financial in character — multiple deprivation, poor and declining physical and mental health, loss of motivation and interest in life, attempted suicide, threat of eviction, poverty and debt. There is a strong social as well as an economic case for the readoption of full-employment policies.

So just how is the jobs programme to be paid for? The government has access to a number of sources of revenue — taxation, borrowing, charges and, during the 1980s, the proceeds of the sale of public assets. Tax receipts for the past two years have been unexpectedly buoyant and have exceeded all official and unofficial forecasts. Indeed, for 1988 it is anticipated that more than £5 billion is available for one or more of tax cuts, public-spending increases or cuts in government borrowing. If the present Conservative government is at all interested in the relief of unemployment then the whole of this taxation largesse should be used in job-creating public expenditure. Of course, this is not being done for reasons discussed elsewhere in the book. So at least £5 billion is immediately available, with much more to come from growing tax receipts. In its public-expenditure plans the government is also allowing for unprecedentedly high levels of reserves: this is money that appears as spending but is not allocated to any particular spending department or programme. These reserves are scheduled to rise from £5.5 billion in 1987–8 to £7.5 billion in 1989–90. It is entirely appropriate that £5 billion of the already budgeted-for reserves be used to finance the jobs programme. So, without changing any taxes or increasing government borrowing, £10 billion has been reallocated to remedying unemployment. But additional revenue is required from tax receipts and through borrowing to fund the programme in its early years, before the additional tax receipts from a low-unemployment economy start to build up.

It would be possible (just) to fund the rest of the jobs programme through increased borrowing. A build-up over three years could be absorbed by financial-services institutions at home and abroad and by household savings. Government borrowing expressed as a proportion of national income or public spending is at such a low level (and the intention is to bring the borrowing requirement down to zero) that increasing borrowing by £5, £8 and then £14 billion by the third year is a possibility. The housewifely economics of Mrs Thatcher and the monetarist dogma practised elsewhere in her government suggests that borrowing for whatever purpose is an evil to be avoided at any cost. Mrs Thatcher herself is fond of likening the British economy to some fictional household, where expenditure never exceeds earned income. Of course, such an analogy has more in common with the financial plight of many unemployed people than with the average British household. The mortgage and consumer-credit boom of the late 1980s demonstrates clearly enough that borrowing is rampant, for the purpose of house purchase, buying new cars, or video recorders, or holidays or just to boost general household consumption. Indeed, we might rightly become concerned if the British government did borrow at an earnings-to-borrowing ratio so common among the leafier parts of the country! So, increasing government borrowing by a maximum £14 billion *could* be the final instalment in paying for the jobs programme. It is proposed here, however, that government borrowing be increased by only £6 billion, and in the first year of the jobs programme.

Increasing tax revenues, job-creating use of reserves and an increase in government borrowing will therefore fund at least £16 billion of the jobs programme. As people get back to work and tax revenues continue to increase in a growing economy, then the shortfall between £16 billion and the £24 billion required will become smaller and smaller. Remember too that the social security bill for the unemployed will also be shrinking.

The final element in the revenue-raising schedule are those that are, and will be, unpopular with the electorate and currently find no favour in Downing Street. They are also deflationary. They are concerned with tax reform. At present, individuals or married couples can offset their mortgage-interest repayments against income tax up to a maximum £30,000 mortgage. Originally introduced as a way of encouraging and subsidising home ownership through the tax system, it served its purpose well. Now, however, it is anomalous, with a 70 per cent level of owner-occupation and growing, and with the highest earners gaining most from the tax relief (it delays their movement into higher tax bands). We have seen child tax allowances and allowances for life insurance abolished. Mortgage-interest relief remains. It should be phased out over a three-year period. For the basic rate taxpayer with a mortgage of up to £30,000 the taxman effectively pays a quarter of the mortgage. Of course, as house prices have increased and income tax rates fallen, the actual value of this interest relief has become less and less to householders. But the loss to the Exchequer remains immense: £5 billion of income tax revenue is foregone each year because of mortgage-interest relief.

Phasing relief out over a three-year period presents no great difficulty. In the first year mortgage-interest relief would be limited to 20 per cent of interest repayments. The £30,000 mortgage maximum would remain. In year two, the percentage relief would be cut to 12 per cent of interest payments. And in the third and final year, a 6 per cent limit would apply. Thereafter mortgage interest would be paid gross by everyone with a mortgage. Administratively, since the vast majority of mortgage payers do so through the MIRAS scheme (Mortgage Interest Relief At Source), this phasing-out over a three-year period is a simple affair.

To illustrate: a £30,000 endowment mortgage with, say, a 12 per cent interest rate costs £300 a month gross. With mortgage interest relief, and a basic tax rate of 27p in the £, as in 1987, the net amount paid to the building society or bank each month is £219. In the first year of limited interest relief, this monthly amount would increase to £240. In the second year, the repayment would be £264. In year three the payment rises to £282 a month, before the abolition of mortgage interest relief altogether and a mortgage payment of £300. This gradual phasing-out of mortgage interest relief would be relatively painless for home-owners, and yet by year four would be yielding an extra £5 billion a year in tax revenue.

The effects of this change would be many. It would help to

dampen down somewhat the enthusiasm for escalating house prices in London and the south-east, where claims for the maximum £30,000 relief are most common. The additional £5 billion returning to the Treasury, when used in the jobs programme, would involve a redistribution of resources from home-owners to the unemployed. It would ensure that home-owners would no longer effect a 'leakage' of capital out of their appreciating housing asset into consumption, partly funded by the taxman. Building societies, banks and other mortgage lenders might in future be more vigilant in their scrutiny of mortgage applicants, since of course monthly payments will be higher. It would clean up a taxation anomaly. Mortgage interest payments for the unemployed should be returned to the basis whereby interest is paid from day one of unemployment: this change being one of the least attractive of the government's incentive measures to get the jobless back into employment. Consumer spending by home-owners will be affected by a change of this kind, but the phasing in proposed would minimise the hardship effects. It would certainly not be harmful to the balance of payments, since the money raised would be spent on the relief of unemployment. Infrastructure spending, including extra spending on housing itself would be the main beneficiary of the extra tax revenue.

The second tax reform proposed also involves housing. Gains made from the purchase and sale of owner-occupied property are currently not included in any tax net. They should be. Labour mobility would be assisted by the dampening down of house-price increases in low-unemployment areas, one effect of taxing the capital gain on housing. Increasingly, housing is being used as a vehicle for investment. This is fair enough, but it is anomalous to tax other capital gains but to exclude housing. In future, capital gains tax should be levied on owner-occupied housing, with an offset for repair and maintenance costs. This would raise an estimated £3 billion a year, to be used on housing investment and infrastructure work.

The capital gains tax would be paid when the gain is realised, that is on the sale or transfer of the property. Normal capital gains tax allowances would apply. So, in 1987–8, when gains of up to £6,600 were tax-free, a property could have appreciated by this amount, plus any spending on maintenance and improvement, *before* any liability to the tax would arise. (This is provided that there were no other taxable gains on items such as stocks and shares.) On average, then, an owner-occupied property could be appreciating in value by something over £7,000 a year before any of this new tax would be due.

At higher amounts of capital gain a year, the normal capital gains tax rates would apply. A majority of home-owners would find themselves not liable for any capital gains tax at all when they come to sell their property and move house. As well as raising £3 billion a year, and having an effect on house price inflation, especially in the south-east, the allowance for maintenance, repair and improvement could well improve the quality of the owner-occupied housing stock.

The maths does add up. An extra £6 billion a year would be raised from government borrowing. The £5 billion currently allocated to the reserves would be used for job-creation. Additional tax revenue building up to some £5 billion over a three-year period would come from the phasing out of mortgage-interest relief. A further £3 billion would be raised from capital gains taxation on housing. And an initial £5 billion, but growing, would come from tax receipts from income tax, value added tax and corporation tax. Further *savings* would come from reductions in social security spending on unemployment, and further tax revenue would accure from a high-employment, growing economy. This budget for full employment errs on the side of caution in ensuring that there would be more than sufficient funding to pay for the complete jobs programme. Planning should commence immediately on the mechanisms for cutting unemployment to a million, and the financial implications of such a change in policy. All the measures proposed should start by 1990, with a five-year plan of expansion and consolidation. By 1993 all measures will be at the necessary capacity, and by 1995 unemployment would be at 3 per cent. The funding arrangements proposed also leave the door ajar for the possibility of further income tax cuts in the 1993 to 1995 period!

The jobs programme, then, is viable financially. Indeed, in estimating the additional revenue required, a positive decision was taken to err on the side of pessimism. There is no good reason for thinking that the radical measures proposed would not tackle the crisis of unemployment in the 1990s. There are no nasty surprises in store from the jobs programme. It would work, all that is required is the political will to implement it, and to restore the return to full employment as the single most important objective of government.

CONCLUSIONS

This book has been wide ranging. There is evidence enough that unemployment in the United Kingdom remains at crisis levels. We have turned our backs firmly against the maintenance of high employment as the most important role of government and its people, and in so doing have equally firmly turned our backs on four million of our fellow citizens. The nation is now complacent about the lot of the unemployed, not wanting to hear the cries of deprivation, poverty, ill-health, and despair. Not even, it seems, prepared to listen carefully to sensibly structured ideas on just how we can substantially cut unemployment. There is a whole variety of ways to cut the dole queue, ranging from the traditional to the novel. Many can work.

This book contains a careful review of the causes of unemployment, necessary in order to understand how best we might remedy the crisis of unemployment. It highlights the vulnerability to unemployment of particular groups in our society, and the difficulties they face once unemployed, and the hopelessness with which they attempt to find work in the late 1980s. There is certainly a range of special employment measures in existence aimed at assisting some of the unemployed in some ways, but these are temporary palliatives, thrown to the hungry unemployed like condemned meat. They take the unemployed out of the official count and salve the consciences of politicians and those in work alike.

The cost of the jobs programme is manageable, the revenue to pay for it all is available to us. Unless we are prepared to write off the futures of four million of our compatriots and one in nine of our children's futures, then work on getting the country back to work has to start now.

'All I want's a job.'

(Chrissie Todd in
'Boys from the Blackstuff')

Selected Further Reading

Aldcroft D. (1986) *Full Employment: The Elusive Goal*, Wheatsheaf
Beveridge W. (1944) *Full Employment in a Free Society*, Allen & Unwin
Charter for Jobs *Economic Reports*
Coates K. (ed.) (1986) *Joint Action for Jobs*, New Socialist/Spokesman
Department of Employment and Manpower Services Commission *Action for Jobs*, available free from Jobcentres
Her Majesty's Stationery Office (1985) *Employment: The Challenge for the Nation*, Cmnd 9474
Her Majesty's Stationery Office (1988) *Training for Employment*, Cmnd 316
Layard R. (1986) *How to Beat Unemployment*, Oxford University Press
Lonsdale S. (1985) *Work and Inequality*, Longman
Minford P. (1985) *Unemployment: Cause and Cure*, Basil Blackwell
Pilgrim Trust (1938) *Men Without Work*
Robertson J. (1985) *Future Work*, Temple Smith/Gower
Williams S. (1985) *A Job to Live*, Penguin

Index